RESONATE

Copyright © 2018 By Alex Wolf LLC

All rights reserved. No part of this publication may be reproduced or transmitted in any form or by any means, electronic or mechanical, including photocopy, recording or any information storage or retrieval system, without written consent from the author.

Cover photography by Diahann Williams
Cover Design by Sofia Cope
Typeset by Chapter One Book Production, UK

For more information, visit www.alexwolf.co

RESONATE

for anyone who wants to build an audience

ALEX WOLF

Dedicated to my generation

CONTENTS

Introduction	1
Chapter 1 – How Resonance Impacts the World	19
Chapter 2 – The Science of Resonating	32
Chapter 3 – How a Resonating Message Makes You Feel	41
Chapter 4 – Why Knowing How to Resonate is Valuable	48
Chapter 5 – The Loneliness Epidemic	58
Chapter 6 – Art vs. Entertainment	72
Chapter 7 – Explaining the Four Elements	82
Chapter 8 – Honesty	86
Chapter 9 – Vulnerability	95
Chapter 10 – Accuracy	103
Chapter 11 – Passion	112
Chapter 12 – The Three Actions that Build Audiences	123
Chapter 13 – How a Message Spreads	141
Chapter 14 – Branding and Resonating	153
Conclusion	166
Notes	174
Acknowledgements	176

INTRODUCTION

I grew up with a dad who got into the internet before everybody else. He has stories about me using a mouse for the first time, which I don't remember because I was two years old. I do remember watching a Spice Girls VHS in my bedroom when I was four—not the official movie, more like a behind the scenes video that followed them as they shot music videos and got mobbed by fans. It was better than the movie in my opinion, I felt like I really got to know them. I was an only child, and like so many of the children from my generation, staring at the screen made me feel as if I had friends. At the end of the video the Girls showed an address where you could send fan mail. I remember the scene. They were all sitting in a mail room with chunky platforms and tube tops, envelops stacked as high as their exposed belly buttons, asking me in their British accents to send them a "lettah". When I asked my dad to help me write one he said, "Why would you send them a letter? Just email them." This was 1996.

The drama in my house was not about what dolls I could and could not play with. It was me begging my dad to have an aol.com email address. He already had dozens of domain names by '97, and all his email addresses linked to those—not AOL. So when he gave me an email address it had the "family domain name". I didn't even realize this was an issue until a few kids in my 3rd grade class started getting email addresses too. At that point I'd had no one to email except the Spice Girls. My friend's email address was something ridiculous at aol.com. I couldn't wait to give her mine but when I did, she looked at me as if I'd told her something in a different language. "Oh my god, this is wrong!" She laughed. "It needs to be at aol.com, dummy!"

I was only eight but my little body ran hot with rage. I knew she didn't know what she was talking about, and I also knew that I wouldn't know how to explain it to her. I went home to ask my dad if I could please have an aol.com address. "Why would you want that? It's just an advertisement for AOL. You have your own domain name. Trust me, it's better."

It's not better because the kids at school are making fun of me. I was supposed to be the girl who knew about computers and here I was being called a "dummy" for knowing more about them before everybody else. My dad raised me to be an early adopter, like him, and that ended up putting me on the outside before I even had the chance to understand what the inside was. But it's okay, because outside is where it's clear I am meant to be.

I remember the comfort I'd feel rushing home from school to melt down into my "office chair" so I could play with Microsoft Word and Powerpoint. Finally, time to be free. I would look up at the screen and feel my forehead relax as I faced the blank pages and all the little buttons on the side. It soothed me to know there were still so many buttons whose function I didn't understand. So many buttons, so many things to learn. And when I would figure out how to do something as simple as change a font or add an image to my document, they were discoveries that felt like little gifts, little treasures. Just for me.

Pressing buttons is how I've learned almost everything, it seems. When I was nineteen and I dropped out of college because—oh my god, who came up with *that* joke?—I went online to press some buttons. The button "Search" proved to be helpful. I used it for phrases like "Is college a scam?" and "How to start a business". I pressed more and more buttons until I knew which buttons I needed to build a website, or edit a video. Buttons, buttons. Figuring out what this one does and what that one does and then one day someone pushed my button in that dreadful excuse for a city, Los Angeles, California.

"Forget TV!" I was at a pitiful event with wannabe stars in a building attached to a strip mall, each perched in a black folding chair, attentively listening. One of the pitiful wannabe stars was me. I was living in the Bay Area at the time and took a $15 bus overnight, sleeping in the most uncomfortable position my body could handle, to make it to this "seminar" *How To Be A Host.* The flyers were sloppily spread all over the fake wood table. The woman who was running it was a "host expert" who helped "stars" like so-and-so from season five of *The Bachelor* get gigs. There was a picture with her and Khloe Kardashian in the lobby. I roll my eyes when I think of it now, but to my twenty-year-old self, I was in the promised land. I wanted to be a star. Fame, fortune, I wanted it all. And like so many young American girls, I was convinced that if I could get that — well, you know. All my problems would be solved.

I weighed about 99 pounds at the time and if I saw 100 on the scale when I woke up, I would skip breakfast. Breakfast was a grapefruit. "Forget TV" says the host expert. "Everything is about social media." All the desperate wannabes scribbled down what was probably going to be their only notes for the year. "People aren't watching TV anymore, they're online!"

She managed to scream for the entire seminar; talking to us in the tone of an annoyed mom who's tired of answering questions. I glanced around. A lot of these girls looked like me. Young, dumb, and too skinny. She continued, "Tweet everyday!" The word *tweet* left her mouth like she used Twitter once a year. I would know. I spent half of high school cutting class, tweeting on the couch and eating chips while my dad was at work. But wait a second, was she really telling me that getting on TV wasn't the answer to all my problems? Was it really about being online? I could do that.

On my way back home, my mind was zooming. Halfway between Los Angeles and the Bay, I made a new Instagram account and started posting quotes. They were quotes about being a young, confused woman just trying to make her way as a business woman, an "entrepreneur". Some of them were funny. Some of them were real. All of them were mine.

The first day, I got 100 followers. The second day I had 200 followers, and by the fifth day, I had 500 followers. I couldn't believe it. There were 500 women who felt like me?! A few years later, the account turned into an internationally recognized brand with followers that now total up in the millions.

While it grew, people sent me pictures of tattoos with my words, posters with my words. I found my words in some of the most random places on the internet, and even on billboards in New York City. No credit of course. People would email me weekly asking with panic "DID YOU KNOW THEY STOLE YOUR QUOTE?" Yes. I know they stole my quote. I wrote it two years ago. I don't care. It's the internet. They steal my quotes, I steal their pictures. They steal my entire brand concept, I steal their—wait. What? The plagiarism is annoying, but I don't care about that as much as I care about making stuff worth stealing. What's more exciting to me is watching how things spread. Organic sharing is a stunning thing to watch take shape. It's a pattern that lives amongst us like a separate being, with waves and lines that if you trace with your finger, looks just like us. It breathes.

Of course, I eventually became completely overwhelmed with the brand and sold it to new owners as soon as I could. During those years I broke up with my American craving for fame, prettiness, and excessive wealth. It was during that time that I realized I'm not a business person. I'm just a person who knows a lot about business out of necessity; I'm completely unemployable so I needed to learn how to make money on my own. I have business *skills* and I can *do* business things, but business *people* are a different breed. Wealth is their alchemy. They get a rush doing the inexplicable, like hiring actual human beings and leading them. I have a hard enough time talking to one. They also get a rush watching their money swell up into ever larger amounts, and never feel a need to stop. I love them for this, but for me, the rush stopped pretty early. While all my new business friends were out there making cash cash cash, I was going to the park or writing poetry under my covers. They were buying Porsches, I was buying paint. Something was up.

INTRODUCTION

"Alex, you're an artist." The words fell out harshly, like a three year old tipping over her LEGO bin. Fun to her, but loud as hell to me and I didn't want to hear it. It was my friend of five years speaking. She knew me well and had the nerve. Her hair was bunched up in a messy bun, and she was eating grapes which added to the nonchalance of it all. That's not a word you just go swinging around. *Artist*. And I don't think I said anything in response, because she was one of the most creative people I knew. If she said it, I figured it must be kind of true.

But it couldn't be true! Everyone knows me as a business woman! Some of my friends are millionaires. Forbes this. Fast Company that. She spit out the seeds. "Alex. It's okay. *God.*"

She was annoyed. I was annoyed. She didn't understand: *I didn't want to be an artist.* To me, "artist" was a fancy word for "broke". I knew because duh, who did you think I was hanging out with? The most creative/broke people I could find. I live in New York, so I hang out with the singers and the actors and the rappers and the writers. I'm a total groupie. You're trying to live your creative dreams? Call me and I will come adore you. But me? *I* couldn't be an artist. What about the money?

"Alex, you're a business person." He was rushing to another meeting and I could tell he was talking to me through his headphones. My friend of three good business years (which is like six regular people years), listening to me whine about my fears, as always. This is what business friends do. "But, but—" he knew where I was going. "You're an artist and a business person okay? I gotta go."

He hung up. Jesus Christ, can someone pick a side? I don't like when things get too complicated. One year I only wore black and white because the thought of wearing colors overwhelmed me. Shit. Maybe I am an artist. I sighed and looked over at my computer. New email.

"Hey Alex, I just wanted to say that I've been following you since you started and your words always resonate with me. Sometimes it feels like you write the exact things I'm feeling and it helps me when I'm having a bad day. I just wanted to tell you to never stop writing. Thanks."

Resonate. That's a word I've heard before. I typed it in my email search box and out of curiosity, clicked a button. Flash. Hundreds of emails from random people who've used that word to describe their feelings about my work. I don't say this to toot my own horn. Fuck the horn. I was finally starting to get some clarity.

INTRODUCTION

When people asked me what this book was going to be about, they were like "So it's a marketing book?" And I was like "Technically, but I would call it more a book about human nature." That's what marketing really is.

By the way, why are you asking? What is it you really want to know? I have to ask because since I've grown that audience online, I've been asked non-stop how I did it. People never like my answers. *Consistency* I say. They roll their eyes. *Good branding* I say. No one really knows what that means. That's fine. The truth is, I can't answer it via email or over twitter because it's an answer that has very little to do with me or whatever supposed talents you think I have. It has to deal with the human condition, and it's something which is long enough to fit inside of a book, so here you go. And for the record, you can get away with skipping some of the most popular books on marketing if you replace them with ones on psychology or anthropology. There are patterns in human nature, pretty obvious ones, and if you pay attention to them you can see see how pathetic and predictable we are.

I've watched messages crawl and spread throughout society in the most creepy and revealing ways. The internet is in my blood and the way things spread on there is in my blood too (God help me). Not only have I seen how they spread, but, because I've been doing this for a while now, I see *why*. When people find a message that emotionally resonates, whether it be a classic novel or a silly motivational quote, there's a strong, complex reaction, one as much physical as it is emotional. *A positive involuntary experience* to be exact, and *that*, that right there is what builds audiences, starts movements and influences culture. Not lil ol' me. Over the years, I've studied how this reflexive reaction plays a role throughout human history, and in here, I've written my observations down. It turns out there's some sort of order in the chaos of getting people to feel united enough to become an audience. An order that, when executed with enough precision, can make meaningless whatever algorithm Facebook plans on using to take over the world.

The other reason why I want you to think of this as a book about human nature instead of one about marketing, is because *duh*, I made it for artists (designers, writers, creatives of all types). I can't just go calling it a marketing book all willy nilly. I need you to actually pick it up and read it. There's not many words most of you hate more than "marketing". Maybe just "responsibility" or "taxes". Wait. Everybody hates taxes. Just — don't worry, okay? I'm not going to turn you into a sleaze ball. You're still going to be authentic when you finish, I promise. This book is about how I think I did what I did. How to get people to really *feel* your work in order to stimulate organic sharing.

Hopefully after reading this, you will become a

millionaire. And if you don't, you can at least use what you know to create a loving audience. An audience you can depend on to live out your dramatic, desperate, artsy dreams. I know this because after my friend hung up on me I realized he was right. I *am* an artist/business-person thingy. And as you can see, I tried to ignore that for the first quarter of my life. What a waste of time. That's the thing about being an artist. If you are one, you are one, and there's nothing you can do about it. You can try to trick the world by hiding it behind a law degree or a busy marriage. You can try to convince yourself that your daughter's paint is only for her and not for you at three AM when everyone is sleeping. You can resist the urge to write down notes about people who would make the perfect characters for your book. But for what? Do you really think you have the capacity to hold in the force of art? You're funny.

"I became an artist and thank God I did, because it's the only profession that celebrates what it means to live a life." This quote escaped wrapped in love and tears from Viola Davis' mouth, as she received her award at the 2017 Oscars. Right after she said it, or maybe as she was saying it, I screamed "OH MY GOD!" at my television and with no warning tears immediately collected on the bottom of my eyes.

As I set out to write this book, I sat down with painters, writers, designers, and thinkers to slurp from their wild, eccentric brains. Every time I told them this quote, they would buckle over, or moan in satisfaction from its blend of truth and poetry. Sometimes I even got to witness the quote drop down like a bomb. Not seeing the words actually hit them until one or two seconds after I said it, catching their eyes squeeze shut as they prepared for impact. Messages like this hit us in a place deep inside, and it's as if we have no control over ourselves down there. It's so weird. We've been given this human body and, like a device, there is so much we *can* control. If you want to move your arm, you can move your arm. If you want to blink, bite, or chew. It will happen. You are the pilot to the ship of your own body every day. But then there are times when you're not. Like when you fall in love, even if it's completely uncalled for or quite frankly—inappropriate. Or when you try not to cry at the movies but Disney manufactures a way to make it happen. There are these moments when something else shoves you out of the pilot seat of your own body for a second and takes the wheel. It's brief, but unforgettable. What is in control in that moment? Who knows. That's for another book.

This book is about how to generate those feelings with your work. Because if you can figure out how to make people have a positive, involuntary physiological response

INTRODUCTION

to it, you will be a star. <u>You will etch dents into human history itself. It is the ancient road to success.</u> We the people go wild when things make us feel good, and at the rate the world is going, sometimes we are happy to just feel. Anything. At all. When messages make us feel, we become raving fans, protectors, warriors, and students of that work. This is how strong messages have always lived, and how they will always live from here on out. Realness, in art, is a wall that we keep trying to hit. Not the realness of the world necessarily, but the realness of ourselves. When we laugh, we feel real. When we burst into tears, we feel real. When our hearts ache with love, we feel real. The trick is finding and making the stuff that will do this. <u>This book is about making that stuff; creating work that reminds people they are alive.</u>

Before we begin, there are two things I want to say. First, this book is not for creatives who still feel glamorous about being in their starving artist phase. You know what I'm talking about. Artists who take pride in their poverty and pain. We all go through it and then some of us grow up. *draw in the sand* <u>This book is for the artists who are ready to eat now.</u> Artists who are comfortable about the idea of having a brand, and a tribe of fans and customers, but who just need a little help understanding how to do it. This is for creatives who are tired of swallowing a gulp of envy every time they see a mediocre artist having success on social media, because in your opinion, your stuff is better. It might be. But I'm going to show you why being better isn't what makes the difference.

As Kanye West so eloquently put it in 2012, "The music industry got hit by a fucking glacier—by the internet." He's right. But it wasn't just the music industry, it was every industry and there's a whole new set of rules now. Being better can only get you so far. And that's why this is not a traditional marketing book. Marketing is not what you have to know. This book is about something you already love and crave to understand more and more about each day: humans.

The second thing I want to say is that this book will be equally valuable to artists as it will be to business people. It focuses on the thing that they both have in common: <u>the need to build an audience.</u>

I will be using some words in this book that I want to make sure you're clear on:

1. The "Message"

This is simple. I use the term "message" to represent the information you want to pass on to the world. Your message can be in the form of written words, visual art, film, music, dance, fashion, or any medium that can be used to spread information and/or emotion.

2. The Creative/Artist

When I refer to the "creative" or the "artist" in this book, I'm talking about you. I'm talking about people who think in colors and talk in songs. I'm talking about people who slip through institutions like butter slips to the other side of a hot pan. I am talking about people who are living in their aunt's basement working on a novel and, oh my god, the novel might actually be a hit and you can move the hell out of there. I'm talking about people who need to make a living from their art because there is no other possible way they can fathom playing any type of normal or traditionally constructive role in society. You and I, we did not come here to work, we came here to play, and we will try to get away with it for as long as we possibly can.

3. The Audience

All creatives have an audience to collect and please. When I use the term "audience" in this book, I simply mean the people who have shown up to appreciate and understand your work. The audience is the people, your people. The people who will rant and rave about you. The people who will buy from you. These people are awesome. They make money and if you do a good job, they will give the money to you. That's what you can hopefully learn how to do well once you're finished with this book. The audience is your salvation. Not only do they pay for you to live, but they give you little envelops of love to place your heart into everyday. They give you a chance to have intense human connections by opening up their chests and allowing you to sing in there, or write in there, or paint in there. And artist, as much as you appreciate the money—that is the real thing you crave. That's the stuff money can't buy.

4. Brand

Brands in the context of this book is how I will refer to entities of emotional and monetary power. I will talk about powerful big brands that are taking over the world. I will also talk about the brand of you.

5. Resonating/Resonance

You've been warned. I use the word "resonate" about a million times in this book so be prepared to read it a lot. And when I use it I don't mean it as a simple sweet feeling. What I mean is a literal physiological experience where:

a)   Something in your body feels like it moved

INTRODUCTION

b) Something on your body really did move (goosebumps, smile, tears, etc.)

Don't ask if erections count. You can gather those conclusions yourself. *Ha!*

So let's get started. My name is Alex, I'll be your guide. Your guide to what? You tell me—hopefully something good. Hopefully something that inspires you to make meaningful things, beautiful things. Things that, while the world might only be half-way working, remind us that being here is still worth something.

humble...
yet knowing &
matter of fact.

CHAPTER 1

How Resonance Impacts the World

As I was sitting in the Uber, it occurred to me that I didn't know what the hell I was doing. I had just spent nearly $100 on a dead, seven-foot tall tree. The driver was turning corners slowly so that it wouldn't slide off the roof. Me and my boyfriend at the time planned to actually bring this thing into our house. On it, we were going to latch sparkly gold ornaments and string twinkly white lights. I stopped by Whole Foods earlier that day and picked up some eggnog and candy canes. The Pandora station was set. The ugly sweaters were on. And somewhere in the back of my mind was a question that kept asking to be answered: *What the hell are you doing?* There it was, nudging me. It wasn't a judgmental *What the hell are you doing?* Though, maybe it should've been since I had only been dating this man for eight months and we lived together and were buying a Christmas tree. That's another story. It was more of a curious *What the hell are you doing?* A genuine desire to know. A valid interest as to what made me feel so compelled to participate in such an illogical tradition. A dead tree? In the house? That you put stuff on? And for some reason it gets me giddy inside? It made no sense but it felt so right. And here we begin to see the first traceable powers of how resonance slithers through culture and shapes our world.

Emotionally resonant messages influence the nature of humanity because they're the messages we save and the messages we live by. You need to understand their influence on you and your life outside of your own creative work. It's more than just finding a few words on a page that feel nice when you read them. It's what humans use to connect, change, and invent philosophies. Emotionally resonant messages have shaped the cultures of the past and will shape the cultures of the future. It's not a message you hear or see, it's a message you *feel*. When humans instill passion, vulnerability, and effort into their work, it sinks into our bones. Hairs stand, tears form, chills travel. Our bodies react. We feel a rush of meaning embellish us and push open a wider lens onto life. These feelings make obvious our universal relationship to each other. As the famous literary genius Leo Tolstoy wrote, *"A real work of art destroys, in the consciousness of the receiver, the separation between himself and the artist."* Resonating messages have the power to heal the pain of isolation, even if you're alone. Even in the darkest of spirits, they can spark a light. → *like Midnight in Paris on the plane*

To see this, you need to use an anthropological eye. You need to remember that we're a species that requires connection to feel alive. These messages do more than just make us feel good on a Tuesday night. They make us feel good collectively throughout the course of history. They enable deep relationships back and forth through the poor to the rich, the ugly to the beautiful, and the dead to the living, all without them needing to be there at the same time.

Depending on what you're into, you could argue that emotional resonance is a communication not from ego to ego, but from soul to soul. A divine transmission of sorts, which would explain its sensational capabilities. Sensational, literally. They rub over our skin and let butterflies loose in our stomachs. When it happens to enough people, enough times, society changes. People create movements when they feel moved. You can trace each cliché, each law, and each speck of wisdom back to men and women who broadcasted messages that vibrated in their towns and were picked up by the antennas of the people.

Every leader, great and evil, understands the art of emotional resonance. They would need to. It's the social formula that captures attention and locks loyalty. Every war fought, every quest taken, every religion made had, on the front end, a face that proclaimed messages that resonated and which spread, influencing thought. The resonance itself is morally neutral—meaning it can be used as a deadly weapon or a helpful tool. It can cause people to kill or cause people to love. Either way, the power in it gives people a cause.

No matter how interesting an idea, in a world like today's, if it's not delivered in a way that resonates with an audience, it will be completely ignored. But messages that *do* can create a cultural current strong enough to last lifetimes. Why? Because messages that resonate don't die. They inspire a social fidelity and get passed down from generation to generation. Inherited like noses and hips. They might change over time but they don't really go away. Most of them live on longer than us. They hover our civilizations close enough that it feels like we're one, but we're not. They are their own entity. We the people are just the vehicles they use to travel.

These types of messages have a gravitational pull that can suck in forces way bigger than you. Depending on how powerful they are, entire families, towns, or even countries can get swallowed into the influence of a resonating message; pounding and rinsing populations around like they're in a washing machine, sometimes for centuries. To underestimate how much control they have would be dangerous. Whatever people resonate with gets treasured, remembered, and preserved. Preserved is the important part because they're so powerful, they can last past the point of comprehension to even its own preserver. We don't have to understand why things are important to *feel* like they're important. All we need to understand is that for some reason it was important to people before us.

One day at brunch I noticed a worn copy of the autobiography of Frederick Douglass sitting in my friend's Chanel purse. "I thought you hate books," I said.

"I don't hate books! I just don't read them," she said. "I found this on a bench and, I don't know, I felt like I couldn't just leave it there." She tucked it in further inside the bag and said, "I just knew there was something about it."

I smirked. The "something" about it is that the book's an American classic and it would seem cruel to ignore the historic context it has by leaving it on a bench. That's what made her pick it up, and now it's in her house somewhere. Who knows if she'll ever read it or not. That's kind of the point I'm making here. She sensed its importance and preserved it not because she planned to read it, but because she knew *it meant something*. That psychology is how resonating messages get shoved and stored inside the nooks of our culture. It's how I ended up buying a dead tree to put inside of my house. The orbit of emotional resonance can curve culture to a point where you don't even know *why* you're doing what you're doing, but you know it feels right. You know on some cosmic plane it appeases the people who have lived and died before you.

But when you actually take time to peel these messages down and try to understand why they're still here, most of them offer a gallery of wisdom and philosophy that give context. Context that reveal things you have in common with humans who lived in an entirely different world than you. Heartache today is just the same as heartache from the 17th century, if it weren't we wouldn't still be studying Shakespeare. Organizing men in times of war now is similar enough to that of the 5th century BC, or else lieutenants wouldn't keep a copy of *The Art of War* in their desks. As American intellectual James Baldwin put it, *"You think your pain and your heartbreak are unprecedented in the history of the world, but then you read. It was Dostoevsky and Dickens who taught me that the things that tormented me most were the very things that connected me with all the people who were alive, or who ever had been alive."*

The human condition has been the human condition since we got here.

If curiosity does happen to prick your little fingers, you can use the archives that the people before us kept as a map. They can help you navigate the meaning of life or ask important questions like: *Why? Why did you want us to save this? Why does it matter? Why did you save these words? This art? These traditions?* It's almost like someone from the past kept them to tell us: There was something about this. There was something about this that was special to us. It might be special to you. Look at it again.

Yes. Ask 'why?'

Because resonating messages articulate the human experience in an almost clairvoyant way, they act as a basket of cherry-picked identities just waiting to be picked up and worn. The misunderstood and the lonely dip inside and find they now have a selection of poems, books, music to express themselves, and they don't have to feel so crazy about being who they are.

We underestimate how much of a relief it is to use artists, movies, writers, and brands to fill in the blanks when we say things like "I am a fan of . . . . ." Or "I'm a . . . . . kind of person." That one line, that one declaration of intentional association, can reveal so much about us and who we are. It makes life easier because we use it to position ourselves in our communities. It's what we use to dig holes in the sand and plant our flags to notify the others where we are.

As you sew your creative work into the world, you'll be stitching in hubs of interests for people to crowd around and enjoy together. It's the story behind the lovebirds who met at their favorite concert, or the best friends who met at their favorite author's book signing. To create a work of resonance means you're making a language for people to represent themselves so they can better connect with each other.

Resonating messages also give us more than butterflies, they give us balls too. They play a huge role in the activity that is normally extremely difficult for humans to do: change. Potent, its ability to shift paradigms comes from just a few drops. When swirled into the pot, it activates wake-up calls. It demands new respect for neglected responsibilities. They are the messages that make dads stop smoking and moms quit yelling. They are the messages responsible for the the moments that sear our experiences with such profundity that you feel like you must change not because you want to, but because you have to. Because you just realized something that you can no longer ignore, have seen something you can't un-see.

HOW RESONANCE IMPACTS THE WORLD

Just as the earth turns, societal norms turn with it, and it's always the artists who can see the shift in the clouds from a mile away. You can depend on the creatives of the town to perk their ears up like wolves when a change is coming. They will dig their paws into the ground and prepare themselves to pounce upon any shift that's drifting towards the status-quo. The writers will write. The painters will paint. The singers will sing. <u>All of this to tell the rest a change is on the way. The creatives like to let us know first.</u>

    All this art then makes cultural space. Space for the citizens of the time to step inside of and feel welcome; get themselves acquainted. In this space, the citizens feel heard, considered, empowered. Eventually enough people will join the space and it will leave a large enough ink blob on the culture that it can't be ignored. The status quo will have no choice but to grow around it, like bark over metal. It makes culture grow a few inches and adapt into a new normal. You can see this pattern play out with the hippie movement of the 60s, the punk movement of the 90s, and even the renaissance/enlightenment period of the 17th and 18th centuries.

In the bold nights of the late 80s, somewhere in the dark, artists like Madonna and Janet Jackson, though probably in different locations, could smell a whiff of 90s sexual female empowerment in the air. The women's sexual empowerment of the 90s would have to be different from that of the 60s or 70s. It of course had to be a step up from the 80s in a conscious and responsible effort due to the AIDS epidemic. Almost as if on schedule, Salt n Pepa debuted their number one hit "Let's Talk About Sex" in 1991. A year later, in '92, the world was introduced to an artist who went by the name of "Left Eye", because that's where she promptly placed a wrapped condom. All of the sudden, Oprah was talking about sex and divorce on national television, a platform never used for that before. Pamela Anderson's breasts doubled in size by 1995, and a new female rapper named lil' Kim dropped her first album "Hard Core" in 1996. All of this cultural space started to form.

Then, some time in 1998, a new show kicked the cracked door wide open. HBO piloted a show about four modern American women making their way through love and life in bustling Manhattan during the nineties. Unlike any other show in the country, it depicted the characters having sex. Lots of detailed sex, and lots of unapologetic sex. The show was called "Sex and the City".

Within months it took off and transformed a nice chunk of culture, validating the space for, not just anyone, but the modern American woman in particular, to be "sexually free". It did this by creating characters and scenarios that only she could relate to. Jokes that only she could laugh at. Only a woman like her would understand them. The show made space for her, and told her story without her having to say it herself. It quickly created a new marketplace and ripped open a new wave of social permission for this lifestyle. The show resonated. Fashion trends set off. Droves of bachelorettes in Manolo Blahniks rushed to New York City, and women felt a little less crazy for being who they were. And just like that, a new cultural norm was born.

RESONATING MESSAGES WORK LIKE THIS:

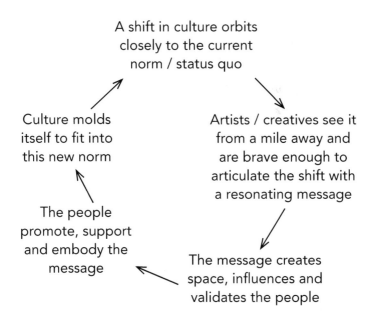

Resonating is not just about you getting goosebumps. It's about the world getting goosebumps, and it changing as a result of that. The work you are about to make is bigger than you. If it resonates, it will be used as the permission that people are too afraid to give themselves. It will be used as a knife to cut through the binds that people need help making their way out of.

So what resonates with you? What does the sensation feel like in your body? How have the things you've resonated with influenced or changed the world? The next time a message resonates, let it sink in. Let the pores of your bones open up so it can settle amongst the marrow. Be observant of how your body changes, how your mood changes. Think about how these sensations work on a collective level, in a society. Think about what these sensations will do not only for your audience but for your life.

> *"Art is not, as the metaphysicians say, the manifestation of some mysterious idea of beauty or God; it is not, as the aesthetical physiologists say, a game in which man lets off his excess of stored-up energy; it is not the expression of man's emotions by external signs; it is not the production of pleasing objects; and, above all, it is not pleasure; but it is a means of union among men, joining them together in the same feelings, and indispensable for the life*

and progress toward well-being of individuals and of humanity."

– Tolstoy

[handwritten: So... What resonates with you?]

CHAPTER 2

The Science of Resonating

I apologize in advance for any Indians that I offend as I tell this story. I should let you know that I love Indian culture, and I love Indian food. Lamb vindaloo was on my Seamless history for months. But as a kid, I couldn't stomach Indian music. I remember this one time my dad took me to a fancy Lower East side restaurant with his friends.

"Take your hands off your ears!" he said, embarrassed. I didn't even realize I was covering my ears. It must've happened as I walked in.

I was six and didn't know what the hell was going on. We just got off the F train and the next thing I knew, we were in this really dark, colorful restaurant. Our table was on the floor, lit up more than the rest of the space.

THE SCIENCE OF RESONATING

Inching closer and closer to it made me nervous. I might be making this up, but I think there was a belly dancer that glittered in the dark as I got closer.

There was this sound playing. This weird, weird sound. Every time my dad would dart his eyes at me to finish my plate, I would reach for the fork, take a bite, and chew anxiously. I had never seen Indian food or smelled it before in my life. The colors of the food and the table were hard for my eyes to process because they all blended in together. "Take your hands off your ears!" Shit. I did it again? I quickly slipped my hands off the sides of my face and readjusted my legs. I was sitting on the floor with a bunch of adults, some of them quite large. My dad was yelling at me. My ears hurt. I wanted to go home.

A week later, I heard my dad talking to his friend in the living room. "I think I know why she was covering her ears." He laughed. "I read online that the Indian music scale is different. It's something about the tones or pitch or something. I think her ears had a hard time processing the sounds, but oh my god, I was so embarrassed." Yeah, yeah, what else is new Dad.

I share this story because it's about vibes. Good vibes. Bad vibes. And even scientific vibes. Sorry, we can't talk about resonance and not talk about the science. It's a scientific term.

According to the rules of physics, resonance is *a phenomenon in which a vibrating system or external force drives another*—Blah, blah, blah. Okay. Each object around us, glass, computers, even our own organs, everything; everything in nature emanates a frequency. If something emanates the same frequency as one of these things, resonance will occur, and it will cause the object to oscillate. Oscillate is just another fancy word for saying "swing" or "sway". If you've ever experienced an earthquake, you are probably familiar with that swaying feeling of oscillation.

Let me give you an example of resonance in physics. Let's say there's a wine glass. If you tap the side of a wine glass with a tuning fork, you can measure its frequency. Let's say the wine glass is emitting a frequency of about 700 hz. You can get this wine glass to "oscillate", or sway, by playing a sound at a frequency around 700 hz. If you do this, you will literally see the edges of the wine glass wobble as it reacts to the frequency being played. If the volume of the speaker is high enough, and the sound waves hit the glass just right, it will move or even be shattered by the frequency alone. If you tried to play a sound that was really loud but wasn't at the same frequency of the glass, it wouldn't break. It's not about the volume of the sound as much as it is about the frequency. Remember that.

Now, before you start springing your new age theories to all your friends about resonance, I need to draw a clear line between scientific resonance and emotional resonance. There is no scientific proof that emotional resonance causes people's organs to "sway". In fact, if our body parts were to actually experience the resonance of physics, it could be harmful. Your liver could burst. Your head might explode. But I don't mean to crush your new age dreams. The good news is that for what you're doing, making art, it doesn't matter if people's stomachs are really moving or not. The point is that it *feels like it.*

This is why as a species we've decided to use the term "this really 'resonated' with me" to explain the impact of art, even though it's a physics term. The definition can still be used with an emotional context and make total sense. It feels like something inside has shifted or was struck like a bell. It's why we say things like "that moved me". Something inside really feels like it moved!

Creatives and thinkers have been keen to this internal sense of vibration that we get from art and have tried to articulate it in the best way they could. In his work *Concerning the Spiritual in Art,* the Russian painter Wassily Kandinsky references famous Belgian playwright Maurice Maeterlinck and his use of words to create sensations. Kandinsky says, "Even a familiar word like 'hair', if used in a certain way can intensify an atmosphere of sorrow or despair.... He shows that thunder, lighting and a moon behind driving clouds … can be used in the theatre to create a greater sense of terror than they do in nature." In *Brave New World*, novelist Aldous Huxley writes, "Words can be like X-Rays. If you use them properly, they'll go through anything. You read and you're pierced."

Even though there is so much left to learn about emotional resonance from a scientific standpoint, the way it works in physics is still a perfect, almost creepy, analogy with how it works with our own emotions. We don't resonate with messages the louder the volume is, we resonate with them the more precise they are, the more that we feel like the stimulus (book, music, art, fashion, whatever) is on the same wavelength (*hehe*).

As far as an objective explanation, scientists don't really know what's going on. There are theories about emotional resonance being a result of some sort of neurological stimulation. An effort the brain makes to piece together what it's experiencing, and how it relates to its past experiences. It's interesting, because there *are* obvious responses provoked when messages resonate other than just our "feelings". I mean, goosebumps and chills are measurable reflexes. Where are those things coming from?

Then there are theories like the idea of "quantum entanglement", a concept discovered by Einstein. It's when two particles come into contact with each other, vibrate in unison, and then separate. The weird part is that after these particles are separated they're never the same, and if something happens to one of the particles, the other particle will also react to it no matter the distance. The vibration of one continues to affect the other, that's why they are "entangled". They have a mysterious,

THE SCIENCE OF RESONATING

invisible connection to each other even if they're on opposite sides of the universe. Einstein called it "spooky action at a distance". I can see that. When you emotionally resonate with something, it feels like you and that message are connected forever. Even if you happen to lose track of the book or the picture that you once loved, it's still archived somewhere within you, and your heart still beats with an appreciation for it.

There's also something called "sympathetic resonance", which even though it sounds subjective, is still entirely scientific. The best way I can explain it to you is if you had two identical tuning forks positioned next to each other. If you struck one of them, it would vibrate. To observe sympathetic resonance, you would stop the vibrating tuning fork you hit by putting your hand on it. Then you'd notice the turning fork next to it, the one that *wasn't* struck, is vibrating on its own. This reminds me of the feeling you get after a performer walks off stage at a concert. You feel both yourself and the whole crowd still beaming bright from the performance. Floating in one big tangled daydream out of the stadium then into the parking lot, where you break apart like a falling firework.

There's even a creepier type of scientific resonance called "limbic resonance". It's an emotionally based instinct nestled in the limbic system used by mammals to be in tune with each other's inner states. Mothers and their children are often the first to experience limbic resonance in order to communicate via empathy and nonverbal gestures. It's a theory that got pushed into further inspection thanks to scientists Thomas Lewis, Fari Amini, and Richard Lannon, who wrote a book called *A General Theory of Love*.

> *"Each time we meet another human being and honor their dignity, we help those around us. Their hearts resonate with ours in exactly the same way the strings of an unplucked violin vibrate with the sounds of a violin played nearby. Western psychology has documented this phenomenon of 'mood contagion' or limbic resonance. If a person filled with panic or hatred walks into a room, we feel it immediately, and unless we are very mindful, that person's negative state will begin to overtake our own. When a joyfully expressive person walks into a room, we can feel that state as well."*

They argue that our nervous systems are not self-contained but rather form themselves in accordance to the nervous-systems by the people closest to us. That explains your daddy issues.

The fact that emotional resonance is still a scientific mystery makes it that much more intellectually arousing to me. Who knows where it starts? Who knows where it ends? Who cares? Just because a guy in a lab coat can't explain it doesn't mean the rest of us can't feel it. Take one look at this species and you'll quickly notice that some of our most talented artists and inventors are completely void of a sense but still have access to this sacred form of emotional communication with fluency. Stevie Wonder is responsible for some of the most emotional resonant art in the world even though he can't see. Beethoven is etched in history as one of the top composers of all time even though he was practically deaf.

A friend of mine told me about a co-worker of her's that had two deaf parents. All four of them were in a car, driving to a skiing resort, and they were blasting hip-hop.

The deaf father goes, "Can you turn it up? I like this song."

The son goes, "Dad, what do you mean you like this song?"

He turns up the volume anyway and then the dad says, "I like it because I can feel the bass."

There was another time I was sitting in the backseat of a car with a baby, no older than seven-months. My friend/her mom, was driving and she put on some music. The baby had these fat, rolly legs that cheered me up on sight, and when the music went on, they moved. Her legs, still unable to walk, legs which barely got her around, swung to the music with impressive rhythm.

"She dances?" I asked.

"What's that?" my friend said as she peeked into the

rearview mirror. I only saw the top half of her face, but a mom face nonetheless. Half-alert, half-worried, but she went easy when she saw the chubby legs.

"Oh my god, honey! You're dancing!" And off she went. The legs moved, sloppily slapping with a delicious innocence against the bottom of her car seat.

What's the scientific reason behind the deaf father loving the bass, or the seven-month-old dancing? I'm beginning to think that might not be the right question to ask. In fact, when it comes to understanding emotional resonance, the power of a thudding bassline and happy baby legs might be all I need to know. Hell, science might ruin it all.

CHAPTER 3

How a Resonating Message Makes You Feel

Resonating messages create emotional fields that suck observers into the present moment and force them to have a reaction, even against their own will, even on a date with a hot guy. Okay, yes—I will tell you. I was at a cafe with this tall, gorgeous man who I felt grateful to spend some quality time with, only because, my generation—we're awkward. Most of us interpret each other through our digital profiles rather than the fleshy, emotional beings that we are. And so when you get next to one of those fleshy, emotional beings in real life, particularly an attractive one who can hold a decent conversation, you don't want to mess that up.

Anyway, there we were, me and this guy. Oh, by the way, I'm a big Jay-Z fan. I have to add that in here. It's just common sense. I'm from Brooklyn. I love hip-hop, the real kind—where the rappers pronounce their words. And while me and this man were sitting down and talking, the barista decided to play Jay's first album, *Reasonable Doubt*. Yeah, bad idea. I couldn't concentrate on a word this man was saying. I know he didn't mean any harm, but everytime he spoke, it just felt like he was messing up the songs.

To respond back to him, I literally had to concentrate. I was tripping over my sentences, because when those songs are on, my mouth is trained to rap with them. Speaking was difficult, almost painful. Talking over that music felt like a waste. All those endorphins, left on the table, I thought. It was like holding in a sneeze. I decided to be honest and tell him that I was having a hard time because of the music, hoping he wouldn't think I was insane (even though I am). He laughed and said it was happening to him too. Jay-Z's music is so good, it messed up our date.

See, that's why these messages are particularly powerful. They're not like the other millions of messages we ignore without thinking about. Resonating messages are different. They provoke involuntary emotional reflexes that make us lose control for a moment. You don't choose to get a shiver of chills, or weak in the knees when you read a book or watch a movie. It just happens. You aren't choosing it to happen. Those moans you send into the air when you read a good quote or hear a good speech, they're impulsive—not thoughtful, and we do them whether someone's in the room or not.

Resonating messages can sink so deep that we don't even need to be "open" to receive them. Usually in communication, the second party needs to be receptive to the message the first party is sending in order for there to be successful comprehension. But with a resonating message, the meaning will hit, even if the second party isn't open-minded about hearing it. [I don't agree] In fact, it's so strong that they could *actively be trying to ignore it* and the message will *still* have an impact on them. This is the embarrassed bow a distant mother makes when she reads something that reminds her she should spend more time with her children. This is the part of the movie the abused person skips, because it reminds them too much of their relationship.

Sometimes resonating messages can feel like they're stabbing you right in the heart, which is why they get so many people to change. They demand that we confront our most vulnerable issues and look at our emotional blemishes under harsh light. But I must say, most resonating messages feel really good, like a spiritual hug. I'd rank it one peg below an orgasm. Especially when they appear spontaneously on a random page in a book, or in the last lyric of a song. They crawl up your back like a spider and leave you with no choice but to inch and squirm as they make their way over your skin. They are not messages you were ready for. They are messages that are ready for you.

And so, when it comes to building an audience, these are the new ways you want to start thinking. Not so much about how to get your stuff out there, but how to get your stuff to make people *come to you* by way of a natural, quality emotional response. Internationally recognized performance artist Marina Abramović says, "A good work of art is like when you're sitting at a restaurant and you have a feeling that somebody is looking at you and then you turn, and someone *really is* looking at you."

It reminds me of this event I was at in Chicago, where Emmy-Award winning comedy writer Lena Waithe was speaking. Some girl in the audience got up asked Lena about her script and how she was having a hard time getting it "seen". That word. *Seen*. It's what all creatives crawl for. That recognition. That respect. And I've always admired Lena's work but her response made me like her even more. She mentioned how she gets flooded with show concepts and ideas everyday. She told us about writers who send emails with forced, eager tones claiming their stuff is the "best", and then she said:

"If you're stuff is so good, then why haven't I seen it yet?"

This raises a bunch of other really important questions you should be asking yourself when building an audience, like: Do people feel compelled to share your work when they see it? If not, why not? Also, how does it perform with the ordinary, everyday person? Do they like it? Do they want more? You want to figure out a way to get the answers to all these questions be yes, yes, and yes. Because when you do, you'll notice that people are talking about your work, sharing it online, and eventually scripts like the one the woman in the audience was talking about will find their way in the dark, in the rain, in the snow, to show up on desks like Lena's. And it won't arrive cold, wet, and unexplained, but warm with adoration from an audience who's already confirmed its value and to business people—its demand.

Well now, this gets tricky because how do you make sure people like it? I mean, J. K. Rowling was turned down by many publishers before Harry Potter was released. The famous French painter, Cezanne, was rejected by gallery owners so many times he destroyed some of his paintings out of sheer frustration. But the thing about these artists is that they were trying to appease gatekeepers, and those people are known to get kind of foolish with those gates.

I encourage you to forget the gatekeepers. Instead, especially in today's world, send your work directly into the vast and emotional void of the people. The standard. The typical day-to-day human, who is dealing with the dramas of love, lust, death, pain, envy, and a small fraction of them, joy, right now. Not a gatekeeper. Not a third-party. Those people are nice and can be helpful, but they also do things like turn down J.K. Rowling, so they don't know always know what they're talking about. They're different than the ordinary, everyday-folk who are just looking for something to ease the pain. Gatekeepers, though still human, use an entirely different angle to gauge your message. They'll tell you they know things, but they're making stuff up. Essentially they just guess. They take a stab about the potential value of your work through their individual biases and profit-based incentives, which have only rusted, hardened, and become out of touch over the years.

The common, everyday citizen is not out there measuring with the same ruler. Instead, they're dealing with fresh emotions, the warfare of moods that comes with being alive. Feeling lonely, confused. Many of them drowning in despair, and who would relish your story about loss, growth, or disaster, if they knew it existed. Others, probably within two miles of you, are giddy on the fringes of a love that's so damn good, no one they know is happy for them. They'd lean an ear to a door just to hear the faint sounds of your poems or songs.

Who needs gatekeepers when there are real live humans out there dealing with life? And you have access to most of them because they're all on the internet, right now. Get over your need for third-party validation. Focus on the real party, the human party, and trust me, third-parties will show up, impressed. I've seen it happen over and over again.

Resonating messages slip through even the most distracting clutter and highest of gates because they activate a raw human reaction. Once you learn how to make them, you don't have to worry as much as everybody else because you're working on a different current of attention. Most people see the surplus of information and they scramble around, putting all their energy into trying to make their message found, when they should really focus on getting it *felt.* Because when the ordinary, everyday-person can find something that warms their cheeks or makes them nod to themselves in the comfort of their own homes, it reminds us that this body can feel. It can sweat, it can laugh, and it can play. And that's a lovely thing to remember, in a world that's going numb.

CHAPTER 4

Why Knowing How to Resonate is Valuable

I'm a horrible person and I like to make fun of people in the street.

"Five," I said.

"Eight! Over there! Look!"

Me and my friend were riding the subway, trying to find the longest row of people looking down on their phones at the same time. It was fun for the first few minutes. There was a satisfying chunk of sixteen standing on the Union Square platform. We laughed. But then we got on the train and everyone, every single person, from door to door, was looking into a screen. Except for one little girl with a pink puff jacket who was staring me right in the face. It made me feel horrible. I counted with my index finger hidden in my sleeve.

WHY KNOWING HOW TO RESONATE IS VALUABLE

"Thirty … nine," I said. And then the game stopped. Me and my friend looked at each other for a few seconds, frowned a bit, and then—we grabbed our phones.

Something is happening in the world and it's freaking me out more than everybody else. The mass selling of attention via advertising business models (television, social media, etc.) is depleting the collective attention span, making it difficult for us to focus on reality, or focus at all. Attention is what you need to build an audience and it being for sale like this, in such quantitative amounts, has sliced our ability to focus thinner and thinner each year. Why aren't we terrified about the consequences of how this is already starting to look? I don't know. A world crawling with humans that can't finish books, articles, or even sentences is already having all types of creepy effects on society.

[margin note: Gary V's attention thesis.]

For example, I was hanging out with an event planner in LA—already my idea of a nightmare, but what he told me was even scarier. There were about three-hundred shiny, curvy people there, and all of them were on full-blown selfie mode. Arms would go up, arms would go down, and clusters of photos and videos were being posted with his event hashtag.

"Wow," he said.

"What?"

"We're getting a lot of engagement with our hashtag. I just checked."

[margin note: Who are those ppl where it's permissible for them to seek/claim our attn w/ their "art"/work vs. those who are "mass selling" or not worthy?]

"That's cool," I said "No one's talking to each other though." I laughed, hoping—I don't know—that we could at least notice that together.

"No, that's how it works," he said. "I learned that I can't make these events too entertaining, or else people won't post as much."

My fingers aren't fat but if they were, I'd point them at the complex entity that is the internet and say: "You! You did this to us!" But it's not exactly true, because we got here by way of our own human nature. It's simple. In a free-ish market, if you can get a bunch of people's attention, other people who sell things—like clothes, makeup or penis enlargement pills—will pay you to get in front of that attention, hoping it gets some of those people in your audience to buy their stuff. So if you want to make a lot of money, all you have to do is make sure people *keep* paying attention. Maybe even get them *addicted* to paying attention, because then you can sell as much of it as you want and make those penis enlargement salesmen pay you forever. This is why social media is free. We are not the customers, we're the products. Well—our attention is the product. It's for sale simply because they're people out there who've mastered puppeteering humanity's unlimited appetite for distraction.

That's why if you focus on what being on the internet actually feels like, most of it is a sad attempt to juggle multiple streams of infinity. News upon news. Updates upon updates. Email, social media, and browser tabs bubble up at rates that cause anxiety if you don't get rid of them quickly enough. These things weren't designed to be finished. You check your feed even when you don't want to, not because something is wrong with you, but because it was designed that way. The bright colors and shapes representing your 'notifications' act with the same stimulation as points in a game, sucking us back into the internet at unnecessary and inconvenient rates. Not only is all this deteriorating our ability to focus, it's making us feel like shit too.

More reports come flying in each year proving that platforms like Facebook and Instagram make people feel worse than we did to begin with. And like all addictions, even though it damages us, we don't stop. We're still here, still scrolling. Even if our eyes roll each time. Even if it makes us feel awful, left out, depressed—each time. I asked a bunch of friends if they could use social media less, would they, and we all agreed: *yes*. We aren't on here because we want to be. Most of us would rather be living real life, sticking our toes in the grass, or, I don't know, falling in love. Feeling torn between wanting the joys of the physical world and being addicted to the virtual one puts a cloud of shame over our culture. It's making us feel stupid and look stupid and I don't think we know what to do. Selling attention like this has made our addiction so serious, we're dying. This year, the amount of people killed in car accidents increased because of people checking cell phones while driving, an obviously irrational and addictive-like behavior. To get off the internet in today's world takes actual effort. Me and my peers constantly try to beat the system. Deleting apps, charging phones in separate rooms, or leaving the house without it just to try to spend some time in the physical world.

The worst part is that instead of coming up with creative solutions to cater to the already sensitive attention span, "creatives" and brands are blasting us with even more bits of information as a way to compete. But if it's the surplus of information that's causing the attention span to shorten in the first place, what do we think adding more of it is going to do?

We are more than just consumers, you know. We are human beings too, and we don't know what mess we're getting into by collectively shredding the ability to focus. The internet is one of the most revolutionary inventions of our species, but you can tell we're new to it since we use it so damn irresponsibly. To pick through the amount of information we come across in a day is literally impossible, and it's training our brains to sort in increasingly discriminating ways. It's forcing us to organize what's worth looking at versus what's not in literal seconds—milliseconds if it can.

Ah, and here you are, the anxious creative, trying to get just a tiny bit of that attention like everyone else.

Hurry up, they're scrolling. What should you do? Should you sing? Should you dance? Should you flail your arms like an idiot and beg for attention? Should you upload those photos from last summer when you were in your bathing suit? Hurry! They're scrolling. That didn't work. Maybe next time.

See, you and these platforms are playing the opposite game. To them, the billion dollar question is *How do we get people to scroll?* To you, the billion dollar question is *How do I get people to stop?* Most advertising companies attempt to get people to stop by trying to capture what I call "zombie attention." It's that lazy layer of consciousness we have when we scroll and we're kind of just there, zoned out. Because remember, most of us show up not because we want to, but because we're addicted. Most of us scroll in the hopes of finding something, anything, that will jolt us from this hazy state, giving us the short dopamine rush which keeps us coming back.

And so, in an attempt to grab our attention in this sad state of mind, people are publishing pitiful, sensationalized content at rapid speeds. Stuff that only gets you to look because it's designed to jab you in the weak spots, mixing an emotional cocktail derived from your insecurities, fears, or sex drive. It's why clickbait, celebrity gossip, and pretty girls do so well with views. Sure, these all get our "attention," but they abuse it. You can feel it. They drain the soul if you get too much in your system.

All of this comes at a tremendous cost, because the majority of us just end up being shouted at, constantly. And right there is where you can see the deterioration of the attention span in action. Because each time they yell, we're forced to sort. Not just through the ads, but all the other pathetic, irrelevant information we get from people we went to college with, old co-workers we stopped talking to, cousins you never liked in the first place, and all other sorts of junk. It forces our brains to make thousands of micro-decisions. *Should I ignore or pay attention?* And no matter what the answer is, just the fact we have to ask is exhausting us. It's giving us decision fatigue, and it's clearly inefficient. Not only does it make it harder to connect to a potential audience, it's making it harder for us to connect *period*. This cannot sustain us. It is not helping us. It makes us feel emptier than we were to begin with, and it can't go on. I am not your zombie.

Everybody just needs to calm the hell down! Brands and audience builders need to remember that we're all the same species here. There are more effective ways to communicate to each other. There are more efficient ways to tell me you have something I might like other than shoving it in my face. If we keep trying it this way, this is going to end up bad for all of us. Just look around. What's the point of building an audience if we don't have a decent society to have one in?

WHY KNOWING HOW TO RESONATE IS VALUABLE

The most important human capability in our history—what's gotten our species to this point, today—is focus. It's what we use to solve problems, create innovations, and listen to the people we love. We need it. If we let it go down the drain, a big part of civilization will go down with it. Whomever has your attention has power, and so we should be mindful about both where it's going and how important it is when you're able to cultivate some. What you pay attention to is in foundational relation to the quality of your life, and the philosophies you live by. What you pay attention to is really all life is made up of. That's why people who know how to sustain, divert, or retain it actually have a lot of control. It's a social tool that can be as lethal as an atomic bomb, wiping out millions. It's why governments and religions shiver when they see it perking up even in tiny meetings or churches. Who carries the torch of attention in a society carries the society. Thinkers like Ghandi, Socrates, and Martin Luther King Jr. all threatened the status quo of their communities with no weapons or armies, just the power to get other people's attention, and they each got penalized for it. Knowing how to resonate is a skill people have used way beyond just "building an audience for your brand." Understand its potency and use it with a steady hand. When you know how to resonate, you are an alchemist of people's focus and decision making. The same attention that makes people get up and do things. The same attention that cultures build themselves around.

Get ready, creative. You're heading into an economy that runs on addictions; an economy that feasts on zombie attention. My advice? Don't be one of the folks using our own human nature against us. Not only because it's heinous, but also because it's just not working. It doesn't matter how much money you have behind your message or how loud you yell it. In the vast void of all this information, it won't matter. We still can't hear you. To be heard these days, you'll have to learn how to talk to a deeper part of us. You'll have to learn how to resonate.

Once you do that, you can whisper and people will still find you. You can spell the word wrong and we'll figure out how to spell it right. You can be far away and we'll make the trip. Knowing this will put you ahead no matter what field you're in, but you have to be committed. You have to be patient, and you have to find beauty in the way humans work. The irony is that the same people who are deteriorating the attention span are already hiring people like you to replenish it. Bigger, clueless brands are on the hunt for creatives who know how to resonate with an audience. They watch their numbers flicker to their horror, realizing that creating the trashiest, creepiest clickbait they can come up with won't bring them back up, or sustain them. It has to happen by creating something that will break us from our addicted, zombie trance. Something that will make those people on the train sit up

> *Haven't we always been this? Except the vice is the thing that's changed?*

and look around. Because to be honest, we are tired of feeling like zombies. We want to feel alive.

CHAPTER 5

The Loneliness Epidemic

So many creatives—perhaps even you—think they're making things for normal people. You know, people who eat three balanced meals a day and drink enough water. People who hand $5 to every homeless person on the street, or wash their hands in their own bathroom. I keep telling them: those kind of people don't exist. Don't make things for organized, perfect people! They're not real. Stop giving out "tips and tricks" assuming that we have the kind of life that allows us to even consider them, or enough emotional energy to care. This stuff, whatever it is you're making, is not going into a fairytale world where people fold their sheets neatly after they've ironed them. The stuff you're making is getting sent into a world where everyone has a backstory. Drama. Alcoholics. Dads who left. Cousins who touched. Moms that died. There is abuse, hatred, insecurities, neglect, and loneliness. A cultural loneliness that's breaking records. Oh, and by the way, most of us are incredibly dehydrated.

Here, I'll go first. It was fresh after a break up, and I just got off a delayed flight returning from a business trip. The delay messed up my schedule and forced me to face the city late at night alone, something I usually try to avoid. Well, especially at that time. The man I had left a few months earlier was one of the ones that thought he could tell me anything. Be careful with those ones. You have to hear their words in your head months after they're gone. The thoughts never bothered me while the sun was out, but at night they would roam with the confidence of roaches.   WOW.

The plan was to get home as soon as possible and try to keep it together until morning. While I was waiting for the train, these little kids were on the platform next to me. Just the fact that they were all different heights gave me anxiety. They were wearing Chinese letters on their backpacks, and rolling all over the place. Their hair was black, shiny, and sweeping in the wind like a cat messing with blinds.

Tired. Lonely. My shoulders felt like horse meat from carrying the bags. I tried to lean on anything I could, close my eyes, and pretend I was home. But I could hear the escalator belt creak and of course, his words. I checked my phone. Nobody texted back. *It's okay* I thought, and felt myself sink one inch deeper into the pain of the night. Nobody knew where I was. Nobody thinks about those things at these hours.

Earlier that day I was in a room with some of the most powerful, rich women in the country. Now I was watching the sign that says my train will be here in twenty-four minutes. *Twenty-four.* The children were using their suitcases as scooters in the best way they could. Dragging them even to the very edges of the platform. Giggling with little terrifying teeth and way too much energy for that time of night. I was too tired to have a heart attack, so I tried to look away. When I turned, I saw the dad.

Attached to his face was a fat, silver camcorder held proudly in the year 2017. He was facing it upwards. The only thing above us was the ceiling of the train station. He had that I-can't-believe-I'm-in-New-York look. I could tell from his jeans, and his suitcase, and his unattended kids. We weren't even officially there yet—the airport I landed in was in Newark, New Jersey. But after seeing him I felt like I was already in New York too. I remember looking down at those filthy subway tiles and thinking, no matter how dirty these get, when I'm amongst them, I know I'm in the right place.

I'm an annoying New York person. People think I've just turned this way but it's always been like this. My parents met in California, and I'm convinced that I was the sperm in my dad's nut sack that urged him to bring his wife and his dreams to the big city. They moved here in '89. Young people who didn't know what the hell they were doing but kept doing things anyway. In '92 I emerged like a pink alien. Translucent skin. Wrinkled fingers. A typical New Yorker.

Finally the train arrived and we all got on. Our stop was 34th street. It was just us. They sat across from me, both the young and old looking out the window. Before I walked out the station, I noticed the lights from the signs outside bounce off the waxed floors and people, so many people, all talking. I relaxed a bit when I remembered life still buzzes around these hours here. It wouldn't be like how it was in California, where the streets are too quiet and too dark to walk around this late. That thought gave me just enough pep to put in my step to pass by the hot garbage and the drunk couples zig zagging down the sidewalk. Sure, I was lonely, but at least I was safe.

But then, even with the stress of the bags, marking my shoulders and hands red, something made me stop right there on 32nd street. Above me, beaming down like a god, was the Empire State Building. It was so quiet but so loud. Around it, an aura of white light that made the sky around it look baby blue. I teared up. *Is this pathetic?* I thought. Maybe. But I was able to ride the rest of the way home completely unafraid of the dark.

RESONATE

How can a steel and concrete building resonate? I have a few theories. It could of course be the idea, right? The Empire State Building. A token of strength, prosperity and manpower for both the state of New York and the world itself. But if I can be honest with you, in my loneliest moments, the energy of New York seems to lend itself as a friend. Everything built here has so much history and energy, I swear to you I can feel it.

In 1929, during the short year and a half it took to build the Empire State Building, the men who welded the highest of the floors were Mohawk Indians. They deliberately searched for high-altitude construction work throughout the Northeast because they believed being that high in the air was a right of passage. Without any gear, they'd walk gracefully across the beams of those skeletal floors, taking on winds that were strong enough to blow them off. Fourteen men died while building it. Joe Carbonelli, an Italian-American construction worker who was still a teenager at the time, remembers the Mohawks telling him, "Joe, look across there. Don't look down, look straight across where you're walking. Put one foot in front of the other, and we'll be behind you if you make a mistake." Maybe that's what I felt too. Something telling me *keep going, we've got you.*

Anyway, I know the Empire State Building is not a

person, but I still felt connected to it. And sure, maybe that's pitiful but it wouldn't be the first time. And that's the point I'm trying to make here. Moments like this make me wonder, what *do* people do when they can't rely on other people? Because, well—how do you want to do this? I can frame what I'm about to say as if you don't already know. Embellish it with statistics and scientific proof, to make it sound more official, or we can just talk about it now because I know you know. The culture! It's suffering from loneliness! Digital connection has become a way of living which has somehow made disconnection a way of life. Gone are the days when there was an "an app for that". There's now an entire social construct *for that,* and it's making us forget how to be human. The only reason I bring this up is because I have news more disturbing than the human race feeling less connected to each other. You know that already. But as a person who's trying to build an audience, you need to know what people are replacing that human connection with, because it will matter to you.

I don't know if you remember, but Eminem had a frighteningly large stake in pop culture in the early 2000s. I don't think even he knew what monster he was waking up, but resonating messages are no joke. You want to talk about positive involuntary physiological experiences? Millions of shithead kids across the country, including me, were laughing, howling, and getting goosebumps while playing *The Marshall Mathers EP*. I probably get more chills today than I did back then listening to the masterfully produced "Stan," one of his most popular songs, released in 2000—the turn of the century, when little angry millennials and young Gen X'ers all over the country saw ancient history where their childhood used to be.

The millennial struggle with identity and loneliness comes from a few things, but one of them is that we got America right as everybody else gave up on it. Our predecessors, Generation X, were fatigued by the nation's desperation to hold on to its starchy traditional values. They grew sick watching it have the audacity to claim a high morality even through the harsh scandals of The Cold War, the AIDS epidemic, and Watergate. They also grew up with baby boomer parents who, while fighting for justice, found enough time to divorce so often it broke records. This brewed the cynical, self-reliant attitude of the American adult of the 80s and 90s.

Some would watch shows like *Oprah* to hear the conversations their divorced parents were too chicken to have, and others had so much fun loopholing the stock market, it crashed. Gen X wasn't like the the baby boomers who had an aggressive desire for change. Gen X said to hell with it and went off to make their own things, like hip-hop and grunge music. They never wanted credit. They just wanted to be left alone. They channeled the pressure to be a good American kid into being a good American badass who questioned authority. They grew up watching *Good Times* and *Happy Days,* but somehow ended up making shows like *South Park* and *Beavis and Butthead*. They were a generation nauseated by the nation's hypocrisy, and who spit out fires as weird as Marilyn Manson and as angry as Kurt Cobain. And how can you blame them? America was easier to believe in when MLK marched around, but for many Gen Xers they were just learning how to walk the same year he was murdered.

So millennials are not the MTV kids, we are the MTV's kid's kids, and that influence got us off to a scornful, rebellious start. Our culture was made up of people who already distrusted society. People who felt misunderstood and skeptical about the world, a perspective we inherited a nice big chunk of. But on top of all of that, what really makes the millennial unique, the thing that makes us a generation of our own is, of course, the internet. Everybody uses it, but it was only my generation who adopted it during the vulnerable ages of 12-18. When AOL and browsing the web in a social way took over, most Gen X'ers were already fully formed adults. And those god forsaken Generation Zer's (the generation after us) only know the world *with* it. But millennials? Can you believe it? We're the only people in the world that grew right by its side.

Nobody really understood what the hell was going

on when the internet hit, but millennials *really* didn't understand what the hell was going on, and there we were, taking it on full speed. Shooing our parents away from those chubby desktop monitors. Loling, brbing, tYpInG LyKke diiS, and of course figuring out how to get access to the world's largest index of porn. Ask any millennial man and he will tell you about the organization he'd put into working around his mother's schedule to look at it. Music? We know it as free. You only bought an album if you really wanted to. Movies? The sole reason to go was to have a place in the dark to makeout. Relationships? We built them through keyboards.

So this type of rapport with the world stained the stems of our first social experiences. Stains I think we can still find traces of in the blooming of—for a lack of a better term—our maturity today. Where one would just have a town or a high school to affirm oneself, we had a gaping black hole of potential identity, the social internet. Your profile pic and screen name was how you identified yourself in the complex, expanding ecosystem of the world wide web—and it took over, *fast*.

I look at it like a technological trifold that happened right at the crux of our adolescence, and it's why I think you hear so many of us refer to our childhood as something that seems farther away than what it is. At that age, when the adoption and cultural domination of the internet grew exponentially, time felt remarkably relative. The contrast in our lifestyle between childhood, adolescence, and early adulthood changed so quickly, we got technological whiplash. And now here we are, left in an era that we did not ask for, where nothing is the same.

It shouldn't surprise us that reports of loneliness have doubled since the 1980s. It's because millennials are all grown up now, and we've been given a society so surreal it plays out like some of Orwell's best science-fiction. In this world, even our parents' most heartfelt advice doesn't work the way it used to, and the idea of living with people who only know an internet world terrifies us enough that we try to go back. We devour the nostalgia of our childhood in amounts large enough to be market opportunities for brands like Urban Outfitters, Nickelodeon, and Nintendo to make money all over again. That's us, trying to salvage the shreds left over from the internet tornado, trying to feel at least a little bit of what time tastes like in our mouths before it melts away again. All this confusion and speed while growing up brewed a perfect storm for resonating artists like Eminem. Funny enough, that's what you can hear in the background of *Stan*. Rain and thunder.

If you don't know know what the song is about, Eminem is rapping mostly in the perspective of a character he made up named Stan. Stan is obsessed with Eminem, and as the song unravels you can hear his affection increase aggressively in the letters he sends to him. He's eager and impatient to hear a response from Eminem, but being the busy celebrity he is, Em doesn't have the chance to respond right away. Unfortunately, Stan loses his shit and thinks Eminem takes too long, so he traps his girlfriend in the trunk of his car and drowns them all by driving over a bridge. Dramatic. I know. But hearing it now, I really had to ask myself why Eminem wrote this. What was he really trying to say?

Julia Cameron says in *The Artist's Way* that "Art's job is to reveal society to itself." In *Stan,* Eminem makes it clear that from his view as an artist, he saw something that maybe the rest of us couldn't. People are lonely. Eerily and disturbingly lonely:

> *See, I'm just like you in a way*
> *I never knew my father neither*
> *He used to always cheat on my mom and beat her*
> *I can relate to what you're saying in your songs*
> *So when I have a shitty day, I drift away and put them on*
> *Cause' I don't really got shit else, so that shit helps when I'm depressed*
> *I even got a tattoo with your name across the chest*

Eminem didn't waste his time making messages for perfect people. He went right for the flawed, the damaged, the lonely, because he knows that's the reality of how we actually feel out here. He knew there was no point in pretending that these big, ugly issues in our society didn't exist. He understands as an artist, acknowledging these types of things is the whole point.

Look, loneliness isn't new, I know that. Every generation has had their fair share of it and suffered. But because of technology and the dark relationship between people and the world, it's a theme in our society in a way it's never been before. And the storm is not over. It's only blown us further apart, looking for companionship in unnatural but adequate ways. People are dizzy from the changes and the pressure. Culture moves so fast. All we want is for a message to reach a hand out amidst the winds of trends and expectations. A hand we can latch on to to confirm for us that we aren't crazy, or that even if we are, it will hold on anyway.

It reminds me of when, as a teenager, I spent a summer working as a camp counselor. It was lunchtime, and this kid was holding an unholy, sticky doughnut covered in pink frosting. "You're really going to eat that?" I asked. "It has no nutrition." But he took a bite anyway, and it's okay—because doughnuts don't nourish you, but they do make the hunger go away.

And that's what I'm here to admit to: We're so lonely, we're replacing our natural capacity for human connection with our own version of pink frosting. That frosting may look like the Empire State Building, or sound like Eminem, and there are some people with money who know this, and will exploit you for it. How I wish it wasn't this way. I'd like to fill this space with a solution that connects us back to each other. I'd like to encourage you and your friends and everyone in the world to look into each other's eyes again, but I'm not going to waste my time. Instead, I'll tell you a short story about the day me and a friend went to go see her mother who lives alone. She's an older woman, and has had a rough life. In the four hours we spent there, we watched television the whole time. And I can't lie, it was nice. We laughed. We talked. We ate. My friend and I walked out right as the Jeopardy theme song started. Her mom was sleeping. "You're not going to turn it off?" I said.

"No. Leave it on," she said. "That thing is keeping her alive."

When you're out there making your work, remember you're not sending it into a world of people who always die alongside friends and family they way it should be—but a world that's not sure if they will. It's not cool that we depend on entities outside of other human beings to feel connected, but it's the reality of the situation. The most important context you can probably have before you even put pen to paper or fingers to strings is that the people are hurting. Kids don't call back, partners have left, blood cells have betrayed. The truth is, people are counting on the thing you make to help soothe those sensitive wounds.

CHAPTER 6

Art vs. Entertainment

There's a certain type of—ahem—creative person that's stubborn. They usually wear whatever's hanging on a *Topshop* mannequin and have a ratio of 5:1 selfies on their Instagram. These people love finding me. They will hunt me down at events where I'm speaking, or ask me out for coffee. Their main goal is to figure out a way to pull me aside and ask, "How do I make people follow me Alex—you know, like you did?" And then a fight begins, because I say you can't make people follow you. And then they purse their lips, because they put so much work into getting me in the corner of this overpriced cafe, thinking this is where I'd reveal all my secrets. And then I swirl my coffee a little bit, even though it's cold now, and I look up at them and think that's too bad, that they're so upset.

ART VS. ENTERTAINMENT

But at least I get a free coffee and I wonder if now would be the right time to ask for a croissant. It usually isn't.

There are a few things I want to say to people like this. Let's start with, *why?* Why do you want so many people to follow you? Is it because your business model needs you to have a bunch of followers to make a profit? Most of them say no, they don't have a business model. Ok. So do you need more followers because it looks cool? You'll feel better about yourself? It's what you think you need? Most of the time, that's what it is. People, especially millennials, think that with an audience comes endless paychecks, a rich supply of compliments to pick at when your ego gets hungry, and last but not least, a nice big wad of personal satisfaction.

But I'm here to say eff all that. Those reasons make me angry. Mostly because I thought that's what building an audience was going to give me and it didn't. Followers or not, I still had to figure out my own creative ways to get paid. Compliments from strangers on the internet are nice, but they don't measure up to the ones you really want to hear from the people you love. Who, by the way, will never give them to you. And personal satisfaction? If you base that on your audience size, it'll work just like the nature of the universe, expanding each time it's reached capacity. This is a bad plan.

I'm not here to show you how to shoot heroin into your ego. I'm actually trying to make the opposite case, that building audiences through resonance is a great, raw way to connect with people. It's not about impressing them or making them *do* anything. Most of it is about humbling yourself. And humbling yourself not because you want a gold star, but because it's how you can bond with other human beings. As you can probably tell, I don't encourage virtuous behavior because I think it'll make you a better person—I'm an artist. The last thing I want is for everyone to get their shit together. If you make yourself too perfect, what the hell will you have to offer the world? Your perfection? Pass.

And so if the stubborn creative person in the cafe has enough patience to hear what I was going to say next, I tell them that sure, you can't *make* people do things, but you can make them *feel* things. And when they feel things, they do things—like follow you. You want to grow an audience? Stop taking the whole thing so seriously. Rigidity and pressure drive people crazy. No one wants to be around that. If we can tell you're desperate for us to be here, we will leave. People like showing up when they feel that you like what you're doing so much, you'd be doing anyway, whether they're there or not.

It reminds me of this breed of stingray that gather on the coasts of Baja, Mexico every summer. Of course they can swim perfectly, but for some reason, they try to fly. They gust up enough momentum under the water with their fins and shoot up and out, into the air. While up there, they flap a few times for good measure and then *splat*, back into the water they go. There's no apparent reason why they do this. But I think it's because mother nature wants to remind us that we don't always have to do things because we should. There's enough room in life to do things because we want to.

People are the same way. It's impossible to convince a group of them to become your audience. Your audience is going to clump up because it's made of people who've convinced themselves. They're convinced that showing up is worth it. That being around you feels good. To do this, you've got to let them roam free. Let them decide on their own what their fins are for. Give them enough room to swim and eventually, they'll fly.

But I think people get confused when I start talking about stingrays in cafes, so I just wait until they show me their profile and say, "Ok. So what do you think?" Most of the time I will look at it and it will be beautiful. A bunch of colorful and high-quality photos. Things spaced out just right. Not one hair out of place. *This tells me nothing,* I think. *I don't know what you do besides take pretty pictures. Oh and post quotes—some of which look awfully familiar, actually.* But I try to say something more considerate like, "What's your message?" "What's your story?" And I close my eyes so I can concentrate on what comes next, but all I end up hearing is a poor mashup of sentences with words like "more followers" and "good content" and I can smell it right there, mixed in with the coffee. They don't want to make anything meaningful. They want a band of worshippers.

Ok. I'm about to piss a bunch of people off, you ready? Entertainment is not art. Both entertainment and art can resonate, and both can build audiences, but they're not the same. Just in case you couldn't tell, there's a difference between Maya Angelou and Kim Kardashian. Kim's body gets a bunch of people to have an *involuntary physiological experiences* so technically it "resonates", and that's why she has a huge ... audience. But it's entertainment, and too much of it is what I think is causing the mess I mentioned earlier. A lonely culture. One where we seek distractions by the millisecond. A society where it's normal to leave the TV on as we sleep, and where I have to frown at little girls watching trainfulls of people staring into a screen.

I don't think there's anything wrong with entertainment. It's fun. It takes the edge off. It gives us a break. What concerns me is that we're using it to distract ourselves from life and our culture seems to have an absolutely horrifying, history-making addiction to it. Because of the endless amounts in which it enters our lives, it seems like all we've got an appetite for. Our palette for amusement seeps down into the food we eat, the news we watch, and the people we vote for, which is dangerous shit if you ask me. The taboo of our culture is not being poor, being fat, or being stupid. It's being bored.

ART VS. ENTERTAINMENT

All this entertainment is numbing us, and making us less equipped to deal with the more serious social wounds of loneliness and disconnection. Wounds that we will eventually need to deal with. Wounds that I think things like art help heal.

A girlfriend of mine was home sick with heartbreak. She had a miscarriage. Her third. I came in with some soup and orange juice and on her nightstand I noticed a postcard with Frida Kahlo's "Without Hope". It's a surreal self-portrait Frida painted with these awful, bloody animals ejecting like vomit from her mouth. It's intense. Months later, I came over and we were laughing, getting ready to go out. I looked at the nightstand. "What happened to that Frida picture? I liked it," I said.

"Oh, I put it away somewhere," she said "You can't stare at those sorts of things for too long."

Entertainment is a band-aid but art is like medicine. We don't use it to block pain, but to help heal ourselves, and it's so strong, you only need it in doses. When we're done, we're done. Entertainment can't work this way because it thrives on constant exposure to stay relevant. But artists like Frida can be dead for decades, not a tabloid in sight, and still have her work sought after by people who want to feel a genuine human bond. Wouldn't you rather your work resonate deep enough to be cherished and remembered after you're dead, rather than forced fed and eventually forgotten about tomorrow?

Real art can do this. It reminds us that we are sensitive, vulnerable, and complicated beings. When we resonate with it, we feel connected. It's a loophole our species has to feel like someone else in the world understands us, even if we've never met. Entertainment does the opposite. It makes us feel painfully separated from whoever made it by way of concentrating on aesthetics and enforcing a false hierarchy. This is most of what you see on social media and television, and it's why it makes you feel terrible.

Most stars in the entertainment industry are not branded to feel approachable or real. Most are deliberately branded to seem set apart or higher than you. They put tremendous effort into looking perfect, and emphasize the least relatable things about themselves, or emphasize relatable things about themselves in the most un-relatable way. The stars and artists we end up really treasuring and remembering are like Frida. The ones who were human enough to show us their wounds.

The reason I'm mentioning all of this is because you can absolutely build an audience by posting pretty pictures on your social media accounts. Our culture has become so visual, people are pulling off whole careers just from eye-grabbing photos and videos. This is the generation that will make Malcolm X's pictures more important than his words, and it's why I hate you all. No—but, this hyper focus on visuals makes young women and men, including myself at a point, think that building an audience is about hiring a photographer and trying to look as happy as humanly possible in all your pictures even if you're a writer or musician and you don't technically need to. You can try doing this if you want.

The girl in the cafe, this is exactly what she was trying to do. Actually most creatives online are trying to do this. They try to get the complexity that is life to fit into well-lit, impressive looking photographs in an attempt to harvest fame just for fame's sake. They want an audience not because they have anything to say, but because they are a part of the same broken, lonely system the rest of us are in, and want to nurse their wounds with praise and attention. So what ends up being made is more and more cheap entertainment. More visuals and distractions that thrive on a false illusion of hierarchy. These build audiences, but they're audiences like Kim K's which resonate by making people think "I wish. I wish. I wish." People resonate with an artist like Frida or Angelou and think "I am. I am. I am." Do you see the difference?

So before you start, even if you consider yourself a pure artist or not, I have to ask: Wouldn't you want your audience to be made up of people who can connect with you eye-to-eye? Soul-to- soul? Of people who will feel as replenished and human by your work as you were when making it?

Because if you're one of those people who want to get coffee and ask me to help you build a following, then this is my official decline. Plus, what do you need me for? You know that all you need to build an audience is to create an involuntary experience. Get started. Follow the footsteps of the highest-selling video games, the box-office busters, and the influencers who play up their beauty and sex appeal. They all sell on account of their ability to stimulate—and dare I say, exploit—the physical body. They do it so well they send you into a different direction, dragging your consciousness outside of yourself. Making people forget where they are, or how they feel. That builds audiences, I guess. But the messages I encourage people to make are ones that send people inside. Ones that bring us back to life. Messages that remind us of what it is to feel. Because those build audiences that even in a world drifting apart day by day, still manage to make us feel connected.

Like that day in November when I closed *I Know Why The Caged Bird Sings*. I was on a jam-packed train heading downtown. It can feel abrupt to finish books while on a commute, especially during rush hour. Pinned to the door, I was immediately and awkwardly caught with my hands now that there was no book to hold.

"Finished it?" an older black male with grateful eyes asked loudly, as if we were the only two people on the train. He wasn't that close; he was shuffled in with about three or four people between us. It hadn't even all hit me yet; that the book was over. I felt my face melt down a little, and nodded with puppy dog eyes, grateful to share this moment with someone. We didn't know each other, but we knew the story.

"Recreational, or for studies?"

After the word "studies" left his lips, I traced out the carefulness of a professor in the arch of his eyebrows. A man who reads. "Recreational," I said, with soft syllables, nervous that I pronounced it wrong. Remember, we had a stage.

"Changed your life—didn't it?"

It came out like a Denzel Washington line, and made the train seem more silent than it was. He wasn't asking me—he was telling me. A long second passed. "Yes. Yes it did."

I felt him push that moment down into me like he was packing flour; grateful he made sure nothing flew away. I walked off the train smiling because Maya is not dead. Maya will never die.

CHAPTER 7

Explaining the Four Elements

I must've been seven, maybe eight, and on my homework sheet was a body full of unlabeled organs. I was able to fill in the heart. The large intestine. The small intestine. It was a quiet Sunday. I was in the living room with my mom. She was reading a book. I noticed a tiny organ beneath the lungs. I interrupted her, showing her the paper.

"Mommy. Is this one the soul?"

Learning the soul wasn't an actual organ was a big day for me. Everybody was always saying how they could "feel things in their soul". And even though I was young, I was pretty certain I had already felt things in mine. I wish I'd been warned. Which is why, before I share the four things that can trick *all of us* into being certain the soul is an organ, I have a few things to warn you:

EXPLAINING THE FOUR ELEMENTS

First, you should know that the following concepts are all ones which you're very familiar with, okay? I didn't make up any new words or invent anything. They're each ancient as hell and that's the idea here. They work now because they've always worked and as long as we're human, they always *will* work. It's about understanding *how* they work and, of course, how to get them to work for you.

Second, even though they're common, they're painful to do. They're so unpleasant, few people are willing to do them. A lot of people want to, but they lack the guts, or the heart. This ends up creating a classic dynamic of supply and demand. Because most people are too afraid to instill these four elements in their work, it rarely happens. Because it happens rarely, people are attracted to it when it *does* happen, and it gets lots of attention simply because it's so unusual.

Honestly, once you learn about them, you might give up on this whole resonance thing. It's okay. I won't judge you. It's not for everyone. Whatever your decision is, I still encourage you to enjoy learning about them either way. There's a lot to appreciate whether you try them or not, because these are the elements that other people, your favorite people, have been brave enough to do in order to connect with you through their work.

Third, you need to know about the love/hate rule. It's pretty simple. Basically when people resonate with your work it causes a reaction, and reactions work on a spectrum. If you flick one end, the other end is going to move too. This means that if some people love it, then some people will hate it. It's the rule. Many artists try to dance around this to be clever, because they think they can figure out a way to be loved by everyone. They can't handle the idea of their stuff being hated. That's fair. It's painful to have your most treasured work treated like garbage. Ouch. Yikes. Yes. But this pain is part of the price. You don't have the power to make everyone love you, and you'll waste your time if you try. Trying to get everyone to love you will only make you hate yourself.

There *is* one loophole to the love/hate rule that'll put you in the clear of harsh criticism and bashing. A lot of creatives do it. It's called fluff. I know you've seen it. They are the cliché, safe messages that get repeated not because someone has anything to say, but because people just want to be "relevant" or "helpful". It's the five million blog posts that suggest ten minutes of meditation will cure your problem (we get it—fucking meditate). Fluff dodges the love/hate rule because it's not loved or hated, it's ignored.

These four elements bring density and meaning to a message. Even if they wanted to, they can't make a message fluff because they act like anchors that weigh it down. They hook and drag messages so low we can feel them in the bottom of our stomach, and in the pulse of our heart.

Lastly, these elements will teach you that contrary to

popular belief, creativity is not a safe space—it is a battlefield. Publishing resonating work is like getting sent into a war and being told that you must take your armor off first. Should you dare be creative and resonate, you will attract enemies who are intimidated by your freedom. Do not come to this battlefield unless you're prepared to defend yourself and the rest of us. So much of being creative is being able to somehow relax in society's straight jacket. There comes a point where you just have to embrace that this is what the world feels like to you today, tomorrow, forever, and create anyway. Artists never really feel free, you know. We make art to get bits and pieces of it, but only because we feel such a lack of freedom to begin with.

I've always pictured freedom as a boundless field strewn with flowers, where the sunshine's so warm you can smell the grass. But over time I've realized freedom is more complicated than that. Maybe there *is* an open field, but you can't enjoy it all at once. The shield that is reality, life, bullshit, gets in the way. But if you're lucky, you can spot some sunshine leaking through the cracks. One ray is enough to get you hooked, but it'll also feel like there's never enough. And that's why we keep doing this. Throughout history, the artists, thinkers, and intellectuals have attempted to put dings in the shield, trying to get more light to shine through. I think the hope is that together, over time, we'll figure out a way to split the whole thing wide open.

CHAPTER 8

Honesty

read in Chris Rock's voice

"Marriage is tough man. Marriage is so tough, Nelson Mandela got a divorce! Nelson Mandela spent twenty-seven years in a South African prison getting tortured and beaten *everyday* ... He got out of jail, after *twenty-seven years* of torture, spent six months with his wife, and said 'I can't take this shit!'" — Chris Rock

Much of the art in comedy is delivering in style what most people are thinking but are too afraid to say. In other words, the truth. When told, the truth can literally stun us. As in—it may cause you to feel stuck, at a loss for words, speechless. It's why we hang up, walk out, and press "block". The truth is like a hot potato, fresh out the oven. Nobody wants to hold it, but because it's so hot, if someone throws it at you, you have no choice but to react.

When a good comedian gets on stage, they expose you, the audience member, to raw honesty. The comedian might say something that seems so private, even to yourself, that you're in disbelief of it's announcement. You feel exposed. This unescapable confrontation with the truth overwhelms your body—it gets nervous, hot, embarrassed—and because it all happens so quickly, you release these feelings through impulsive laughter. That type of response is a high-quality emotional reflex. It's a vigorous energy with the power to vacuum us into the present moment.

Our body responds so strongly and obviously to honesty, we can measure it. When we lie, our heart rate goes up. Our eyes dodge around the room to avoid other eyes. Our voice may weaken or crack. And lie detectors are cool, but if your audience has a gut and a bit of common sense, they'll be scanning for truth with their own eyes and ears, trusting what they feel. Our personal lie detectors come built in, and we use them to sniff out the authentic, resonating messages from the frauds. That's why you, as a creator, never need to worry about copycats. They copy the authenticity, which is not the same as the authenticity itself, and for some reason we humans can mysteriously feel the difference.

And I'm not telling you to be honest in your work because it's the right thing to do or because it'll make you a better person. *Boring.* I'm telling you to be honest because it *does* things. What was once there, after honesty, will be something different. Sprinkle a little on a relationship and watch it curl into a new shape. Try to have some over tea with your family and watch them get up and leave. The truth might as well be a see-saw. You can't push one side down without the other side going up. That's how well it forces a reaction. People might fight it, avoid it, adore you for it, run from it, ridicule you for it. But the one thing humans can't do with the truth is just let it sit there.

Honesty makes the air thick. It creates tension so dense, things feel like they're going in slow motion. It's rejection, unwanted desires, left-swipes, no calls back, failure, racism, hypocrisy, low bank-accounts, divorce papers, death certificates, trauma. If these are a part of your story, don't leave them out. The reason why the truth hurts so much is because it crumbles our illusions. We use those. They patch up our paradigms. They help us sleep at night, and make us shut up and do our jobs. But honesty doesn't care about your job, or your sleep. It will come into the room at midnight banging cymbals and tell you to quit your job right now, idiot. It's all the ugly parts of life. The parts we keep our heads turned to avoid looking at. But there's no point in that, because honesty hovers hauntingly, quiet as the sun, and beams over even the darkest parts of you, sizzling and burning through your deceptions with no mercy.

And I don't know how, but most of us hold our truth inside. We let it shave our organs down until they feel as sharp as pencils; poking the hell out of us each time we breathe, driving us absolutely insane. If the truth destroys things when it's out in the open, can you imagine what it's doing inside of you? The only way we're even surviving is because there's that loophole I mentioned. Resonance.

It's like there are emotional pores that each human has access to. When a person is brave enough to be honest in their songs, in their poems, in their work, the rest of us get to ooze our own gunk out of these pores with them and, like a miracle, it soothes some of the pain. This is what your favorite creatives have done for you. This is why you are a fan. They've made some noise about their honesty and, in silence, you got to enjoy it. You got to watch the show from the back row with shades on. You got to see how the news lands on the world first, without putting any skin in the game. You don't have to tell a friend if you don't want to. You don't have to tell the person you're married to if you don't want to. You get to smile in the comfort of your own discretion, knowing that this is between you and the artist. Someone gets it. Someone gets you. Thank God.

And because of that relief, you've kept them around. You listen each time they talk. You buy a ticket each time they come into town. And you wouldn't have done it if they had been spewing the cheap stuff, the stuff that gathers on the top. You're loyal because they took your hand and dragged you into deeper waters. They showed you that even though it's dark and intense down there, believe it or not, you can still breathe.

And now it's your turn. You want to get followers? Tell the truth. What resonates more? In the sea of dishonesty and agreed upon illusions that we'd like to believe are real, there's nothing more obvious, more pronounced, more noticeable than honesty. It attracts suspicious attention like a feminist at a Trump rally.

The world is covered in secrets that we civilly dance around, tip-toeing until our ankles hurt. Uncover one of those secrets and watch the rest of us crawl all over it like ants on meat. We won't be able to help ourselves. We don't always like sharing our *own* honesty, but we have no problem feasting on yours. And I don't say that to discourage you, because the truth is not something that belongs to you alone. It belongs to all of us. You're not creating it, you're exposing it, and the people who expose it get all the credit.

Unlike other parts of art, you don't have to imagine this part. The truth is already there. It's like cake mix. Most of it is already set up, ready to go, and the ingredients are easy. No creativity or talent required, add those for fun. The main ingredient is something else, something only the *real* artists have: audacity.

It's simple. What everyone else is saying, say something else. Say the one thing people are afraid to say but that is true. If there's a pink elephant in the room, all you have to do is point and say *"Am I seriously the only one who sees that?"* And then people will freak out because they'll say they saw the elephant too, and they're so happy you said something—here they thought something was wrong with them. Wrong for seeing elephants, wrong for feeling shame, wrong for being insecure, wrong for feeling stupid, or liking faux fur or *Legally Blonde* or socks with the toes. Wrong for being who they are, and just by you mentioning the elephant, a wall of crazy crumbles for them. Resonance happens, and they feel better because you just confirmed that they weren't crazy at all. Boom. Fans for life, because now they trust in your audacity and they'll be searching for it as their crazy-feeling life goes on and on. And the good artists are always there, making sure that just in case someone comes checking on them, their fingers are still pointed to the pink elephants in all the rooms no matter how ugly they may be, no matter the hideous shades of pinks in which they may come.

Does this mean you'll have to say things you haven't seen anyone else say, or share things you haven't seen anyone else share? Haha. Yes. I know you think there's no way in hell you're going to reveal this or that. There's a truth you have that's so ugly, it's making you shake right now just thinking about it. You're scared—blah, blah,

blah. So are the rest of us. But it's not the honesty you're afraid of. You're afraid of what it will destroy. You're afraid it'll destroy some people's illusions, maybe people you care about, maybe even your own. But the crash and collapse of those illusions are the exact sounds that create the resonance. There's no way around it. Did you really think you'd be able to make something meaningful without enraging a father or embarrassing a mom? Come on. Get real. All the good stuff—that's what it costs. That's what it always costs.

If you don't break these things down with your integrity, they'll collapse on their own, under the weight of shame. So better get ahead of that crash. Appreciate the destruction, artist. Yes, it might hurt for a couple of days, but you knew that going into it. If the truth is why something falls apart, trust me, it was never that strong to begin with, which might be the other fat pill you don't want to swallow.

I was in the park talking with a friend who wrote a short story that mentioned her mother's abuse. Everyone loved it. Everyone besides her mother. "She said she never hit me," my friend said. "Alex, *I have scars*! I'm so pissed off! When she does this I hate her."

She paused to look at me, mistaking my silence for judgement. "I know it sounds harsh but—"

"Stop." I told her. "It's okay to leave it at that. What if you *are* harsh about this? Wouldn't that be okay?"

She didn't realize she was talking to a fellow writer, and that in fact made it absolutely okay. Actually—that's my advice for you if you're finding it hard to be honest. Don't picture a room filled with your friends and family, who will be the first to say something that will completely throw you off. Instead, picture a room full of cynical, broken artists who are just like you. Who live to hear the truth, no matter how hideous. Because whatever you have to say, we can take it. Artists are sensitive people, but if you really pay attention, the good ones are way more sensitive to the world than they are to other people. I'm not saying you should be a complete asshole, but, you know, have enough courage to use your emotional space. You're entitled to it. You have the right to be angry, confused, or heartbroken, and when you're happy—dammit, you have a right to be that too.

You've got to show us the truth no matter what falls. It's the only way we'll ever get to see what you mean. Destruction is the force responsible for progression. We dissect organs to learn how to live longer. We reverse-engineer the weapons of our enemies to better protect ourselves. We choose honesty to make sure whatever structures we've built in our lives can handle a few shakes and screams. If they faint, let 'em faint. We can't keep pretending like the world is a soft place forever.

When it's all over with, you'll see. Not all is lost. Certain things will have fallen but there will still be a few folks who stood around, and finally you'll feel alive. Because by the look on their faces you'll be able to tell that not only did they love what you had to say, they want to hear more.

So when it comes to your message, what are you polishing? Leave it rough. What are you erasing? Keep it there. Show us scratches. Show us wounds. Even though the truth is ugly, it doesn't mean you are. And it doesn't have to be dramatic. It can be funny or wise. It can be colorful or musical. Just make sure you tell us. Let us see it in your face. Let us hear it in your voice. Tell us how you got to be the person you've become. Describe to us in detail the naivety of some of your bad decisions. Stop thinking about what will sound good. We don't care about that. We care about if you fell in love with the wrong person like we did, or if you don't know what the hell you're doing, like we don't. Because all of us have scars, artist. But if you're the one who wants to resonate, it means yours are the ones we will have to see.

CHAPTER 9

Vulnerability

Honesty and vulnerability are wrapped together so tightly they're often seen as one, but if you twist them apart, you'll see how they're quite different. Honesty is the truth itself, and vulnerability is the emotional *position* the truth puts you in, a position you have to be willing to be in in order for your message to resonate. I'll give you an example. When you fall in love with someone and say "I love you". for the first time, the honesty is the words "I love you". The vulnerability is the nerve-wracking, gut-clenching silence you experience right after you say it, not knowing if the person will say it back. It's not about saying how you feel, it's about accepting whatever happens now that you've said it. A transfer of power, your ego's worst nightmare. It's handing over an emotional dagger to the world knowing they could use it to stab you when you're not looking. Vulnerability is not pain, but being open to the possibility of pain, which can be more frightening than the pain itself.

It reminds me of that scene in the 2001 movie *Baby Boy,* where Tyrese and Omar Gooding force these young men who robbed them to line up in a row so they can punch them in the face one by one. The young men know the punches are coming, and have to stand there and brace themselves. Omar gets in this one kid's face, close enough to feel his breath. He raises his fist, and explains the art of the punch to Tyrese. "You see you gotta get up on 'em real close, draw back—not too far though." Then he points with his gun. "Aim for the nose or the mouth. Preferably the nose, 'cause it's soft." During all this, you can see the kid squirming in fear, knowing his face is about to experience the punch of a lifetime. Watching that scene made me wonder, *what's worse? The punch, or the moment before the punch?* By the look on the kid's face, the suspense seemed more terrifying.

And that's the suspense you have to live in if you want to resonate. You have to allow people to get so close to you that if they wanted to, they *could* aim right there, for the nose. It's the only way people will be able to see how human you are. It's standing defenseless, even if you may want defense, even if you may *need* defense. It doesn't mean you will get hurt, it just means you can. You can get hurt because you are real here. You are honest here.

VULNERABILITY

You are not the mask you flaunt here. If someone wants to stab you with their words or judgements, they won't have to wrestle through any shield or bulletproof vests. Vulnerability means your skin is out; warm, misting, and exposed for puncture.

When it comes to these parts of ourselves, we shield them, callous them, slab a bunch of vaseline and grumpiness on it so that we're less likely to get hurt, and there's some logic to that. It's for survival, a way to protect ourselves from turning into nutbags. Because vulnerability is how trauma happens. Trauma, in its essence, is when something in your life changes so much that you can never be the same. It makes your previous reality so distorted that you have to learn to live with a new one. A reality you probably didn't want to learn to live with, but were forced to live with anyway. And because vulnerability is where we have our thinnest emotional skin, whatever happens there scars. This is why people stay away from vulnerable territory. Scary things happen here. There is lot to lose. This is not just *a* risk, this is *the* risk. The risk we have to take as humans not only if we want to resonate, but if we want to feel alive.

And as with all risks, the deeper the loss, the greater the reward. Vulnerability also happens to be the only place you can go to taste the nourishing and completing power of freedom. True love cannot find you unless you come here. True freedom cannot find you unless you come here.

To seal your life as "lived", to seal your love as "true", you have to enter. It's just the only way. You need to be as visible as a stranded man on an island waving for a helicopter. Visible enough to be saved, but at the same time, visible enough to get shot.

You'll know you're watching vulnerability because it will be impossible to be neutral when you see it. You'll either have a strong desire to stare at it, or a strong desire to look away. Think about car crashes, open wounds, watching a baby be born. These are moments where you're catching people in their most defenseless, and it's a natural trigger for our sympathy. In art, vulnerability can be nerve racking because it can look stupid—pathetic even, for both for the viewer and the artist—if it's done right. But all those perceived weaknesses are the ingredients for the most powerful bonds in the world.

To be able to say "You look stupid" or "You look dumb" to another person when they dance, act, or read poetry is sometimes the main reason why we don't do it. Holding that particular power over them, the power to hurt them, implies a responsibility. There's a beating heart in your hands. Someone actually let you hold it, and it's your choice to keep it intact or squish it between your fingers. Most of us feel honored to get ahold of this stuff. It's a curious experience.

We usually get too distracted by it to consider using it to hurt them. Instead, we look down, asking ourselves *how in the world do I get this energy to pass out of me? How would it feel if I let someone hold mine?* Having this much intimate access to another person's heart makes us realize that we might have the same access to our own.

Most people I've spoken to try to build an audience by creating messages that are as safe and un-offensive as possible. They think that in order to speak to the masses, they must trim their edges and cut their thorns, but of course, without thorns, nothing snags. File your message down too much and you'll end up with a weak blob of "no-offense". To resonate, you have to make something that can be attacked. Not because you want it to be, but because those are the things that force people to feel. If it can't be attacked, then it's not real. It's not human. Everything inside of us, our raw thoughts, our real feelings, never have a smooth finish. They are rough and rigid like crystals. Sometimes sharp enough to prick a finger, but we don't let that stop us from enjoying their natural beauty.

What if they take what I'm saying the wrong way? They ask and I say yes, I know. You have to be okay with some people misunderstanding you. Like when I say, "Are you being dead ass rn?" there's a chance you don't know what I mean, but if you do, you're probably laughing. Resonance. And some people might write me and say, "I can't believe you said that Alex! I am personally offended!" But it's probably because they've misunderstood me. But for a line like that, and the people it connects me with, it's worth it. You see? Resonating messages don't exist to be right. They exist to be real, and real things scare people. That fear might make them want to strike it, but if something is captivating enough to be attacked, then it's captivating enough to be defended.

Learn from nature's most vulnerable design: the infant. It can't take care of itself and it can't defend itself, but it's designed in a way that makes nearly everyone else do that for them—for that exact reason. Its vulnerability. Their skin is so thin, it's see-through. Their necks are so weak, they drag without support. And they come with big innocent eyes that we're compelled to smile into, promising that they'll be okay. They are a living, breathing representation of how concentrated vulnerability awakens the most human parts in us. That sure, humans suck most of the time, but even the really bad ones tend to find compassion for things that can't defend themselves. There are parts inside of you that are just as fragile, waiting to be articulated and shared. Don't put guards over them. Don't scrub them down so that they can be tough enough to handle the jerks and the idiots you're worried about. Because when you do that, you won't be left with a baby anymore, instead you'll have something more like one of those ugly naked troll toys from the 90s. When you pick at your message like that, you're just making stuff for assholes and not the people who really want to hear you. Leave your message bare, susceptible as the infant. Because vulnerability, when it's potent like that, is such an effective trigger for human compassion, for resonance, that it's what you depended on to get here.

After a while, the fears that come with being vulnerable will be less sour. Let the water run and you'll see. It clears up. Most of the fear gets replaced with wisdom, because now you know it's worth the trade off. Now you know there's no point in trying this, any of this, if you're not going to let yourself really feel it.

I'm reminded of that part in the book *The Giver*. The main character, Jonas, lives in a world with no risk for pain, and no room for pleasure. Love and death are outlawed. There is no fire, there is no color. Everything is gray and safe. One day, Jonas gets a glimpse of what the world looked like before all of this, when it had emotional variety. He sees a room filled with a happy family opening gifts on Christmas day. Jonas isn't sure how to process what he sees, but he knew it felt good and he tries to make sense of it:

> He could feel that there was *risk* involved, though he wasn't sure how. "Well," he said finally, grasping for an explanation, "they had fire right there in that room. There was a fire burning in the fireplace. And there were candles on a table. I can certainly see why those things were outlawed.

> "Still," he said slowly, almost to himself, "I did like the light they made. And the warmth."

That warmth is why you're doing this, and you can't feel it without being open to the risks that come with fire. Making your message safe is not your job. Defending your message is not your job. Leave that to the people. Your job, the real reason you're doing this, isn't about making everyone happy, it's because you have a truth to share. The value of your message shouldn't be based on approval ratings, but rather the depth of loyalty you have for it. The willingness within you to stand by its side, knowing that it might offend some and empower others. If people throw tomatoes, you should be able to wipe them off knowing that it doesn't change how you feel. You are human, and this is what you have to say. Expressing yourself means so much to you that they can keep throwing those tomatoes, it doesn't matter. You're going to stand here anyway.

CHAPTER 10

Accuracy

The best way to explain the third element, accuracy, is to tell you about this experience I had in high school. You'll have to forgive me, as much of my time in high school is a blur. The one memory that sticks out above the rest is how desperate I was to get the hell out of there. I went to three different high schools in three different states, which is essentially the same as going to none. During my senior year, my guidance counselor handed me a full schedule with eight classes. On the bottom, in teeny letters, it revealed that I only needed to pass two of them in order to graduate. I chose Government and Art.

All I remember about my art teacher was her frizzy red hair and the concern in her eyes when she'd look at me. I sat at a table to myself, listening to my iPod. Alone and probably stubborn looking, but I accepted her assignments obediently. She couldn't tell, but I was excited. But you can't show excitement in high school. It's against the rules. One time she asked me if I ever thought about going to art school. "I think you'd be a really good fit," she said. I wanted to hug her, but I just stood there with one headphone hanging out my ear and shrugged.

Anyway, one day she passed out these magazine clippings of random objects—phones, chairs, plants. The one that landed on my desk was of a cup. "I want you to clip these to the edge of your papers, upside down," she said. "Then as best as you can, I want you to draw it that way." So, you know, I went at it. This was 2010, so I was probably listening to Kid Cudi or The Blueprint III. I didn't really understand why she was making us do this, and then fifteen minutes later she got our attention and said, "Okay, now flip it over." I did and *holy shit*, I thought. It was the most realistic thing I've ever drawn.

I never would've been able to make the cup look so real had I tried to draw it normally. Artists who've mastered a realistic style of drawing understand how much their own perceptions and consciousness get in the way of making something look the way it actually looks. For people with a less skilled eye, we draw what we *think* we see instead of what's *actually* there. What my teacher showed me was that by drawing something upside down, the bias your mind has about it gets removed. A flower is no longer a flower. A nose is no longer a nose. They now just become combinations of shadows and light. While drawing, your mind can't compartmentalize these enough to apply its common sense. And so, you draw what you see instead of what *you think* you see, and create a more accurate depiction of what's in front of you.

I want to stress again that resonance both in science and with our emotions is all about reflection. The wine glass doesn't resonate from a loud frequency, but a matching one. Unless the frequencies are identical, the resonance doesn't happen. There needs to be a perfect reflection, like a mirror. If you want your message to resonate, there needs to be parts that reflect the people who face it, and does so accurately enough that they could mistake it for themselves.

When we get a good look at our reflection it creates a unique awareness that we're forced to acknowledge. The mirror is where we go to check if that spot on our skin looks serious, if our eyes are still red from crying, or if we've had one too many martinis. We rely on it to get the real story. One day on the train I overheard a man say that crack saved his life. "How?" his friend asked. "I looked at myself in the mirror and couldn't recognize myself."

The mirror, like a resonating message, shows all. A job less emotional than you'd think. Indifferent, it's not here to show you what you think you see, or what you hope to see. It's here to show you *what is there*. It's one of the most unbiased references we have in life, detached from our feelings, arriving as bluntly as medical records thrown across a desk.

Accuracy is capturing the truth with a lack of sensitivity that in turn stimulates sensitivity. Like a reporter who delivers the news with a narrow variety of inflections no matter what the story may be. If the boy is dead, *the boy is dead. It is what it is* and that's what accuracy forces us to embrace. It causes resonance, because when things are said in such plain terms, with a lack of emotion, humans overcompensate for it. We make up for the sentiment that wasn't included in the message. We'll take the stale information, the harsh reality, and animate it with our own sympathy, passion, or rage.

If honesty is the dirt, then accuracy is like the little mouse that burrows underneath it. The feral animal that gets the nitty-gritty. The shards of the moment that are so obvious and ordinary that we can't believe someone caught them. In 2005, on Kanye West's second album, *Late Registration*, there's a song called *Rose*s. He opens it with the sweetest, yet most ordinary explanation of him walking into a hospital to see his grandmother:

> *I know it's past visiting hours*
> *But can I please give her these flowers?*
> *The doctor don't wanna take procedures*
> *He claim her heart can't take the anaesthesia*

ACCURACY

It'll send her body into a seizure
That lil' thing by the hospital bed, it'll stop beepin'

Everything about these opening lines reveals information that doesn't explain explicitly how he feels, yet because of what he's shared, we can tell. But the way he says "That lil' thing by the hospital bed" is where we really get to see the accuracy of his scene setting in action. Even though it's an ambiguous literary description, it's an accurate human one. Think about it. This line wouldn't resonate in the same way if he used the words "heart monitor." And he could've beaten himself up for not being *"articulate enough"*, but he allowed the description to come out of his mouth the way it felt in his heart. Being accurate is not about being literal as much as it's about having enough courage to explain with clarity and precision things as we see them. When people are close to death, we don't see heart monitors, we see "lil' things by the hospital bed". It reminds me of what the famous author Anton Chekhov wrote: "Don't tell me the moon is shining; show me the glint of light on broken glass."

Accurate messages resonate so much because they don't feel like you're being talked to, they feel like you're the one doing the talking. Or rather, as if someone slapped a mouth across your gut and it can speak now. The reason why Jay-Z is my favorite rapper is not just because of his Brooklyn charm, or his talent for triple entendres (those are nice, but …), it's because when I rap to his songs, I never feel like like he's rapping at me, I feel like he is rapping through me.

So much of what he says feels like what I would say, but he combines the words in a way I wouldn't have thought up on my own. So many of his thoughts are thoughts that were floating around inside of me, unidentified. He gave those ideas a voice and put them into clever, energetic lines, with melodies and swag. His music snatches these roaming, unlabeled emotions and gives them all a name and a place. His songs do a lot of emotional organization for me, and this is what good art does.

Even Kanye said, "If you're a Kanye West fan, you're not a fan of me. You're a fan of yourself." And I think it's true for all the artists we love. As much as we appreciate them, it's really because they make it easier to appreciate ourselves.

Most messages are just bad outlines of what people really meant to say. What you get is a trace of the thing and not a depiction of the thing itself, which distances the messenger from the message and therefore the message from the audience. You can't be afraid of that center, the crux of what needs to be shared. As bright and boundless as it may appear, once you've identified it, walk towards it. Tread no further than its membrane, act as a journalist and dutifully record what's there. If it's fuzzy, say it's fuzzy. If it's gold, say it's gold. There is a level of simplicity and elimination you must allow. There is a trust you must have in the clearest of sentences and the most obvious of words. Give them clearance, because we as a species need help articulating the many overwhelming feelings within us, and each contribution helps. When just enough room is committed to the exactness of what you're trying to communicate, with the same audacity as a mirror, you are then playing in the field of masterpieces.

It was Aristotle who said: "The greatest thing by far is to have a command of metaphor. This alone cannot be imparted by another; it is the mark of genius, for to make good metaphors implies an eye for resemblances."

An eye for resemblances can't exist without an eye for accuracy. That eye can spot which separate characteristics of the world mirror each other symbolically, identify that symmetrical symbolism and then position these disparate things together to our astonishment.

If you dare to tackle the ambiguities of the inner world, and then name their external equivalent, it will catch attention, resonate, and spread like crazy. Think about the rapid sharing of the Internet Meme. Memes spread across the web like wildfire because they resonate through their commitment to *precision*. They capture the tiniest, simplest nuances about life. They're so accurate, we can't help but save and share them impulsively.

When you finally get enough nerve to roll up your sleeves and create a resonating message, be mindful that your bias showed up with its sleeves rolled up way before you. It's like when you tell your friend to "act natural", and right away they start blinking funny. Our humanness has a habit of crawling right over us, tainting our ability to simply show what we mean to show, or say what we mean to say.

Perceptions and insecurities come crashing in like waves, eager to get there first. Eager to wash away the sandcastles of your psyche. Dulling them until they become something unrecognizable. And then people give us a description of what's left, the remains, and it doesn't quite resonate. But the committed creator expects these waves of bias and prepares to capture at least a little bit of what's there before their consciousness zooms to shore. To get to the good stuff, you must sit there, patient as a rock, observing with the most objective lens you can push forward. Then, collect enough information about that damn sandcastle so that by the time it's washed away, you got what you needed.

If you can figure this out, how to express with precision the human experience, you're creating mirrors that reflect parts of us we can't see. That's why, of course, these messages are treasured, whether they're a story, a song, a painting, or even a shoe. They place an x-ray hand mirror over our stomachs, showing an articulated version of what's inside of us. This is the closest thing to magic we can feel. Not only is it pleasing and awakening, but it gives us leverage to express ourselves in newer and better ways.

Make tangible feelings that were once malleable as snot, and a burden gets lifted for the rest of us. Do you know how much of a relief it is to be able to take something an artist has made and tell people "See, *this* is what I mean. *This* is how I feel." You will build an audience if you can describe what, for most of us, feels indescribable.

Accuracy puts a finger on things that we couldn't put our fingers on. Like a laser, it cuts out the burdensome emotions that overwhelm us, and gives us a chance to hold them and inspect them at our leisure. Even the most hideous of cysts can be appreciated when sliced off and looked at up close. If you want to resonate, turn what you have to say upside down. Change your perspective of it enough so that it is not what you think it is. Allow it to, in whichever way it needs to, become a blend of shadows and light. Spend some time on it. Trust the process and when you flip it over, *holy shit*. It might be the most resonating thing you've ever made.

CHAPTER 11

Passion

On Wikipedia it says that hip-hop was invented in 1973, but if I was in charge, I'd edit to say it was invented on May 3, 1933, because that's the day James Brown was born. I don't know what kind of sick trick God was playing when he allowed that man to land on planet Earth, but his existence left enough debris in the air that if you sniff hard enough, you could smell him right now.

The fourth and last element to a resonating message is passion. And when I say it, I don't mean it in the cliché, pathetic way of you "finding your purpose" or your "passion in life". Spare me. I'm talking about the raw and intoxicating energy of fervor. The stuff that made Mike Tyson bite through an ear, and made Van Gogh cut his off. It's man at his most supernatural. Where he acts as if skin won't bleed and cars don't crash. With it comes a subtle appetite for fear, pain, lust, pleasure. Anything that will let him taste in its entirety the complex and everlasting flavors of life. That's why we'll start with James Brown.

As you think of him, I don't want you to imagine the man who screams, I want you to think of that scream itself. Even though he could sing your girlfriend's panties off, in his most infectious work he's not singing at all. He went down in history for the way he'd shout and howl, which teaches us that passion is not about *what you say* nearly as much as it is about *how you say it*.

Those sounds he made are not ones he found on a music sheet, by the way. They're roars that cracked off like dynamite from the heat of his complicated strife, resilience, and joy. And it's not just his cries that are made up, but the rhythm of the instruments as well. Not many people realize this, but Mr. Brown was a composer. He invented an entire genre. Arguably two.

Where Rhythm & Blues and Rock & Roll emphasized the second and fourth beats of a bar, James, by trusting the passion he felt inside, dramatized the first beat. A rhythm of one. This made every instrument in his band—the trumpets, the bass, the trombone—get played as if it were a drum, the instrument of the heart. This gave us the sound we now know as Funk. Fred Wesley, one of Mr. Brown's trombonists, remembers: "He'd get the band members to jam together and then one by one he'd get each of them to play what he was hearing in his head."

In his freaking head. This means, essentially, the sound we know as funk is really just a melodic transcription of Mr. Brown's passion. A sound that was so dependable and regenerative that it was used all over again as the rhythmic bones of hip-hop. James couldn't have gotten so funky had he relied on a music sheet! Funk happened because Mr. Brown understood that to make work that resonates, it has to come straight from *the soul*.

Unlike the other three elements, there's an essence in passion that's both genuinely immortal and scary. Immortal, because when you catch a human being talking, dancing, singing, or writing passionately, it seems like if you killed them right there, in that moment, they'd be fine with it. They're those moments in time when you can just tell the person wouldn't rather be doing anything else. That's actually why it can be scary, because it's man at his most cosmically aroused. When people act immortal it forces the rest of us, who take painful caution with our mortality, to go into a paradigmatic sized self-interrogation. It's only when we see others live bravely, freely, passionately that we ask: *What the hell am I even doing with my life?* Not only that, but passion can be scary because it's staring right into a human face and for once seeing how it looks when it lacks fear. An expression which can quickly translate to mania or insanity, like

Heath Ledger playing The Joker. He played the role so passionately, they think it killed him.

It makes sense that James Brown's first influence was the Protestant church. Have you ever been in one of those? They used to scare the shit out of me as a kid. It was the only place I'd see adults jump and scream, and I wouldn't know what to do with myself. The transformation was suspenseful, *each time.*

Women would show up in coral and lima bean colored dresses, and on their heads, hats would sit as slanted and buoyant as Saturn. Gloves in hand, they'd nod and smile to say hello to me and my mother as we walked by. The most cheerful, docile church women you could imagine. Shortly after, the preacher would come out with his early voice, still groggy from the morning. He'd say hello, how are you, and give us points for showing up today. Little by little his voice would get louder, a bead of sweat would form on his forehead, and I don't know how, but eventually the whole room felt like a tilted board game. Those same women who just said hello are now crying and hollering and throwing their hands in the air. One or two of them are on the floor. And my mom is just standing there looking as normal as possible and I do my best to mimic her, but in my chest I could feel it. I'd have to push against the gravity in the room so I wouldn't get sucked up and swept into the back. One more loud shriek from the preacher and I might've slipped right with them. This is what passion does. It makes you hold on. Here you are trying to have control over yourself and by lifting even one of those fingers off the edge of the seat, you're gone.

The good news for all you sinners is that passion doesn't just work at church, it works at the club too. Years ago I saw a man embarrassing himself on a dance floor. People were laughing at him. He was hardly on beat and dripping sweat, but I couldn't take my eyes off him. As much as he looked like a fool, he also looked incredibly free.

I was still a teenager at the time, very shy. Very used to mean New York kids who would humiliate you if you tried to dance without being particularly talented at it. But watching him, I felt like I had in church. All I wanted to do was move. I had to intentionally negotiate through strain to contain myself. I could feel my hip bones begging me to sway to the music, my feet tapping as a way to seep out some energy. Eventually, with the help of one or two more drinks, courtesy of a fake ID, I was able to join the dance floor and finally enjoy myself. Thank god I did, because, as Shakespeare put it, a person who doesn't dance is a threat to society:

> *The man that hath no music in himself, Nor is not moved with concord of sweet sounds, Is fit for treasons, stratagems, and spoils; The motions of his spirit are dull as night, And his affections dark as Erebus. Let no such man be trusted. Mark the music.*

Shakespeare knew that the ability to feel passion was a symbol of your humanity. It works so well in resonating messages, because all you need is a body and a soul to feel it. This is what I'm convinced James Brown understood as he composed his music. You didn't need an identity to get funky. You just needed some arms to flail, and a mouth to make crooked. He knew how to get a foot to tap whether it was white or black, and it's why the rhythms of his music are the most sampled of all time. They work.

And I don't know if I'm allowed to say this, but I think the reason why so many black people are exceptional at nearly every passionate art form is because culturally, we've had to slice our spirits open just to check if they were still there. To feel your vocal chords tremble as you sing the blues, or your hips slide as they dance to funk, can seem like physiological luxuries against a numbing, oppressive society. I'm convinced these are methods we used (and still use) to remember our humanity, as a survival strategy for living in a world that wasn't treating us like one.

But my point is that passion is the energy we can *all* exert to feel worthy when seas get rough, which is why it's so commanding when you put it in your work. It gives us physiological permission to feel alive. It sends out a universal memo letting the rest of us know someone had enough courage to live here and enough balls to feel it, which works as an invitation for the rest us to do it as well.

There is both a tempo and temperature in passion that gets the rest of us to sit up. Sex? Love? Life? What would these be without the heat of passion? In fourth grade, on warm fall days, the wind would blow and I'd catch yellow leaves on the floor trying to spin into complete circles. It turns out wet heat and wind are the ingredients for a tornado. What I was catching was just harmless, underdeveloped ones that weren't going to go anywhere. I now realize this reminds me of most people. Man is a warm fall day, but passionate man is a full blown tornado. Think about the humid circles of bodies that crowded around someone like Malcolm X as he spewed with enthusiasm. I imagine you couldn't walk past something like that without feeling the heat.

Even on cold, dry pages, words written with fiery energy transmit conviction to the reader. The most soothing sounding instruments need great amounts of physical energy to be played, enough of it to break a sweat. Composers, actors, comedians, athletes, there's no way you can picture them at their most resonating moments without imagining their glistening foreheads and fast-paced gestures. Michael Jordan was so passionate about his shots, he'd stick his tongue out. In fact, it was that same passion that got Jordan a multi-billion dollar deal with Nike, which for the logo they decided on an actual silhouette of his body while splayed out in mid-air.

An easy way to tell if your message is passionate

enough to resonate is to check your temperature. You should at least be a little warm. Whatever you're passionate about will send blood swirling all over your body. You'll be able to feel it add a generous gulp into each heart beat or push against the skin of your face.

Another way you can tell if your message is stemming from passion is if you find it difficult to articulate the reason why you're doing it. Since it's such an intense tangle of energy, the second you try to describe *why* you make what you make, you'll probably realize there's nothing to say. Words are a measly device to communicate the power of passion. Louis Armstrong said, "Man if you have to ask what jazz is, you'll never know." And Picasso said, "Everyone wants to understand art. Why not try to understand the song of a bird?"

I learned this lesson from a woman who used to live in my building when I was a kid. Mrs. Keats. Everything in her apartment was red. The rugs, the curtains, the pots, the pans. She only wore lipsticks within the spectrum of firetrucks and crimsons. The only thing that stuck out was her white cat, who's scarlet collar would rub against our legs as we walked inside.

She'd invite us over for milk and cookies every once and awhile. Me and my friend were always mesmerized by her decor, trying to peek under everything we could as a way to challenge both her commitment to red and our eyes to its consistency. But each time we opened a cabinet or pulled a drawer, we were proved wrong.

Being only about ten at the time, we figured that when we'd get older, we'd decorate our places just like hers. It seemed like the right thing to do since Mrs. Keats was so happy. She wasn't like the other adults in the building who would avoid eye-contact. She always used the word "darling", and had the most theatrical laugh. We recognized the other adults in the building more from their coughs and murmurs rather than their hellos, but with Mrs. Keats, we'd always see her coming from a mile away. A beaming red strawberry walking down the block with a graceful wave, dramatized from her over-sized sleeves. She was always happy to see us. She was always happy to see everybody.

One day in August, after serving us milk and cookies on a red Santa Claus dining set, we looked at her and knew today would be the day we'd ask. We were dying to figure out the meaning behind all this.

"Mrs. Keats, why do you love red so much?"

Here I was thinking she'd tell us a long story about her childhood, maybe a dark memory she'd experience during a world war. But nope, it was a curt and mysterious answer which both my friend and I could tell was the truth. She took a sip of tea, looked outside the window, chuckled a bit and said:

"To be honest with you darling, I don't know."

Which is what I think Mr. Brown would've said if I

asked him why he made music, and what Picasso would've said if I told him to explain a painting of his.

What gets you so worked up that other people feel compelled to ask *why* you're worked up about it? Do that. I can't explain to you why culture and technology gets my mouth drooling. Louis Armstrong couldn't explain to you why jazz made him want to skip the streets. *It just did.* So whatever makes *you* do this, put it in your message. Even if you can't describe it, even if it's something you can't explain. Actually—*especially* if it's something you can't explain, because only when you get *that* comfortable with the energetic ambiguity of passion will you finally realize, you're on to something.

FOUR QUESTIONS TO ASK BEFORE PUBLISHING

HONESTY
Does it show/represent a truth that enough people are aware of but are too afraid to deal with?

VULNERABILITY
Are you, as the artist, in a position vulnerable enough that outsiders can say you look or sound stupid?

ACCURACY
Can people identify/empathize with it enough to feel like they're the one who said it/made it/did it or "couldn't have done it better" themselves?

PASSION
Do people get a sense that what you made is something you'd be okay dying while making, if you had to?

CHAPTER 12

The Three Actions that Build Audiences

I was looking over the glass case. Inside were glossy photos of tattoos, some of them very ugly. "Alex, please. Don't do this." My friend was annoying me. I was twenty-two. I knew exactly what I was doing. "Will you just relax?" She was embarrassing me. The guy with the big arms covered in pin-up dolls and skulls was staring at us, and I didn't want to look like a novice.

"So, this is what you want?" he asked.

His hands were bulging out of his latex gloves as he held my cracked iPhone. He was staring at a photo I'd found on Google. A photo of a tattoo of Steve Jobs that somebody else got. I wanted the same one. For the record, it wasn't like a detailed portrait of Steve Jobs. It was a pixelated version, designed by Susan Kare, one of Apple's first graphic artists. It was tasteful, okay? Hipster approved.

"You're going to regret it." My friend made sure she slipped that in between me and this very nice gentleman's conversation. I looked up at his chin. It had three piercings.

"It should be about $120," he said.

Sold! Well, not really. I decided to go home and think it over for a while, and I'm thinking about it right now. Wow. Yeah—I can't fucking believe I was going to do that. She was right, I would've regretted it. What was that all about? What did Steve Jobs ever do to make me consider something like that? Oh yeah, that's right. He resonated.

I remembered this story as I was sitting in a boardroom meeting at this mega-rich company. All the men were in suits. All the women had hair that looked overbrushed and over-dyed. The whole thing freaked me out. They saw my work and had called me in to help them go "viral". I walked in with overalls and vans, still secretly wanting a Steve Jobs tattoo. "We need ENGAGEMENT," this guy said.

Oh, what a lovely buzzword. Buzzes like a bumble bee holding a 1950's vibrator. *Engagement?* I thought. A clicker was in his hand. "Like you see here. This photo got 435 likes. We think it's because of the orange in her shirt. It's more likeable."

That must be it. My mouth was closed.

"Can you show us how you got so much engagement?

THE THREE ACTIONS THAT BUILD AUDIENCES

We need . . . . . . to be big! We've been one of the most valued companies in the country but our social media needs work. We need to connect to millennials."

So I said, okay. I'll show you. And I did. I rolled up my sleeves and told them exactly what they needed to do. I told them about the new American consumer and how they need to resonate with a message in order to be loyal to it and share it. I broke a sweat explaining some of my observations of human nature, and how things spread online. We laughed big laughs, and we smiled, and we poured coffee, and everything was chipper and then he said, "Okay, so, can you show us how to get more ENGAGEMENT?"

Ahem. Dear all my misguided audience builders of the planet, engagement is not—I repeat, is NOT—a measly double tap on a screen. It is not going viral. It is not likes. To make this really clear, I'm going to point out the literal range of physical effort it takes to express what most of the world is calling "ENGAGEMENT". When someone likes a photo or follows someone on social media it involves a literal ½ centimeter wide gesture of tapping your thumb on a screen (usually while in a sedated state of mind).

Now, let me ask—is that what engagement looks like to you? Hmm. That's interesting, because to me engagement looks like a twenty-two year old contemplating getting a dead white man's face permanently tattooed to her body! I guess we just see things differently. And so I stuck everybody in the room a cold middle finger and walked out. Just kidding, of course I didn't do that. I worked with them for a few months and they weren't listening to me so I gave up. And guess what? Their social media still sucks.

It's not easy to get people to do things, you know? People are very stubborn. Look at you. You can hardly get yourself to do things. Yet, here you are trying to get others to like your stuff and follow you and buy from you? Humble yourself, young one! Re-evaluate your priorities. Getting people to make microscopic gestures with their thumbs will not be the sign that you've made it. I don't know why that's the goal for so many people. You'll know you made it when your audience is saving pictures of you as their wallpaper, sending letters they know you might not even see, changing their wardrobe, copying the fuck out of you. That's engagement.

There are three *real signs* of engagement that make audiences, and they do not happen unless a message resonates with a person first. They don't happen by asking people politely for favors, and they don't happen by tricking people into liking photos with orange shirts. They happen on somewhat of a chemical level. When a message opens your gut and grabs hold of your soul, it activates dopamine, and once that's released it's simple. Dopamine hardwires the body like a computer to come back, share, and buy.

These actions I'm going to share are what "engagement"

really is. They are the actions that, when done over and over again to enough people, create an audience and build a brand. They're actions that exist way beyond the boundaries of social media. Likes, follows—those are all just by-products. Audiences have been forming way before they were here, and will be forming again after they are gone. It doesn't matter what happens to social media or technology. The way to build an audience will *never* change as long as the audience you're trying to build is made up of human beings.

It had been years since my Los Angeles fiasco and I wasn't sitting in classes to become a skinny celebrity anymore. I was now on a quest for things more nourishing. Literature, the arts, philosophy. And these classes had people who I could definitely tell enjoyed to eat. This particular day, I happened to be sitting in a writing class taught by the woman who made me look at words differently, Anne Lamott.

She was standing there just like I imagined. Wiry, copper dreads tucked beneath a headband, and that soft voice that I always hear shine through her words when I read them. Her collar bones subtley pronounced beneath her cotton shirt. A shirt I could tell had been washed many, many times. *Good,* I thought *How a writer is supposed to look.*

"If you want a good life, it's simple. Read and write," she said.

The whole class scribbled that line down. If the crest of my couch could tell you, it would, of the mornings and nights I spent curled with her books, crying and laughing into the silence of my living room. Her books have had a way of finding me at divine moments. For example, the day I found *Traveling Mercies,* I walked out the bookstore, still looking at the cover, and right behind me a freshly waxed Toyota Camry crashed straight into the storefront, breaking the windows and totalling the car. Her book kept me seconds away from getting hit.

Anyway, I took a bunch of notes in that class and made sure to snap a picture with her. In the photo you can tell I caught her mid-book signing because in the edge of the frame her hand is holding a pen. *Pinch me now.* That picture, along with my collection of her books, gets special treatment. They're the kind of books that if you happen to be one minute away from packing your shit when you've about had it with your boyfriend, you think, "Those are going in the box first." Because resonating messages cling to your spirit even at your lowest. You can lose your lover, your job, or your mind, but wherever you're going, that message is going with you. And this, this is the first sign of engagement when a message resonates. You keep it.

I actually hate that I have to use this next example because it's so techy and kind of sad, but right now, if you

THE THREE ACTIONS THAT BUILD AUDIENCES

go through your phone, pay attention to your screenshots. Taking screenshots is one of the most instantaneous and obvious examples of how we keep things that resonate, because it's so impulsive and fast. You see something that makes you laugh or sigh and right away, *click*. Start studying what you save. What makes these things worthy to become a part of your personal archive? The effort you put into adding something to the collection of yourself is telling. Pay attention to all of it. We only let messages orbit closely to our hearts if they hold some authentic value to us.

We don't only do this with our phones, we do this with our entire bodies too. It can feel like an anatomical screenshot when something resonates. It makes us go woah, woah, woah—hold on. Let me write that down. I need to underline this. Wait, I need to take a picture. Almost as if we're obedient little drones, the body will buzz us off on a mission to make sure we emphasize the existence of this message in our life. We can't let those ones go by. We have to buy the book, get the album, see the movie, twice. Maybe get a tattoo? Anything to make us feel like it's part of us a little bit more.

We all have memories of our parents whining at us about how annoyed they were during our horny teenage phase, annoyed that we couldn't memorize our math homework as well as we could Usher lyrics. Well, Mom, geometry can't stimulate the newly found hormones racing through my body quite as well as the *Confessions* CD can. And because they did, I've been able to sing verbatim every line and inflection in his song "Can U Handle It?" since 2003. What are we going to do about it now? The geometry didn't resonate, it's gone, but the song did and it's stored. That's how this works.

What's in your archive of life? Think about the physical things you've kept, or stuff you have memorized—they are both examples of keeping. These messages drip juicy, emotional shots of dopamine into the body, which affirms that it must be important, it must be magical, and it must be saved. The fact that you kept them means they make you feel good enough that you can enjoy them when you're alone or when no one is looking. And in a world that honors showing off, think about the power of that type of intimacy. Do your messages have the zing to make people feel that comforted? That understood?

Do people care about it enough to save it? Because my advice would be to try to design these things so people have a hard time throwing them away, like Apple does with those iPhone boxes. They use a lot of subtle tricks like that to make their brand resonate. It's easier for me to toss those boxes away now, but I knew I wasn't the only one who'd kept them around when I noticed one in the corner of my friend's shelf in high school.

"You didn't throw that away?" I asked, pointing at the box with my chin.

"No," she said. "You're supposed to throw those away?"

This is exactly what you want your audience to feel with your work. Give it enough life, enough beauty, that getting rid of it just doesn't come up for consideration. It should be obvious through your effort that things like this are too nice, they were made too deliberately to be thrown away or forgotten about. This makes people decide on their own, not by way of tacky persuasion, that the idea of life without your art would seem less complete.

Back at the writing class, it had been about an hour or so since we got started, and people were getting cranky for a snack. While others went off to get bananas and granola bars, the real Lamott groupies, like me, lined up by the podium. I don't normally get starstruck, but in this line I could already feel my heart pounding. People handed her books, flowers, chocolates. When it was my turn I was flustered, and asked with a frog in my throat if I could have her email please.

"Are you working on something?" she asked with a smile.

Hm. I wasn't expecting this question. I didn't think about it. *Should I be working on something?* I don't know. I just assumed she'd hand an ol' girl a paper and scribble her email address on it. But I just stood there and realized eventually I'd have to respond.

"Uh, no ... I just ... I just wanted to stay in touch." I said.

And then she gave me those eyes, those darling, soft eyes that I know were there when she wrote all those darling, soft words, and said, "I'm 63." She laughed. "I'm tired. I'm sorry."

I could feel the people behind me. They were close enough to hear what just happened, and close enough for me to tell they were eager for their turn. I immediately went from being the sweet-eyed Lamott admirer to the annoying fan who wasn't getting the fuck out the way. I don't remember what I said, but I scurried off quickly because I didn't want to cry right there in front of her. *How could I have been so stupid!?* I thought. *How could she have been so mean?* I stood in line, now at the food court, sizzling each time it got shorter. The whole class felt different now. I was humiliated. I felt stupid for even asking. I almost didn't want to go back. *She couldn't just write her damn email down?* I remember it hurt swallowing that banana because my throat had closed up from the embarrassment.

Class continued. Of course my chair was in the front row and I was now mortified to even let my face show in the crowd. I knew she'd see me in her peripherals—the intrusive, psycho fan. She spoke. I looked at her, thinking about how emotional this relationship has already been. *What did I want her email for anyway?* I thought. I didn't really have anything to say. I wasn't expecting her to help me with any connections. I let out one of those self-laughs, the ones where you look down a bit and shake your head because I realized in that moment: *I guess I just wanted to be friends.*

But see, that's what happens after a message resonates, first you keep what they make, and then you go looking for more. It's like when you're eating a bag of chips and one is not enough, and two is not enough, and before you know it, the tips of your fingers are covered with pointy crumbs and salt and you shake them over your mouth as your head is tilted back and you feel like an animal and you're thankful no one on the train is really looking.

Yeah, Anne Lamott was looking, and she didn't want me touching her with my greasy fingers. That's fair. She layed a boundary. It was honest and blunt as hell I thought—but it was fair. Everybody probably wants to be her friend, so she has to draw the line somewhere and above all, she was gracious and kind about it. I don't need to be Anne Lamott's friend to get the best out of her. I just need to be her reader. But my brain tricked me into thinking that if I could just get her and I to have slumber parties where we paint each other's toenails, life could be even better than the books. This is what resonance will have you thinking.

But there's beauty in this sort of thing, because if you really think about it, it's the birth of the organic search.

It's what send us off into a pursuit of our own interests. It makes us read movie credits, take time to skim the archive, or buy the rest of the collection. Google is just the engine but resonance is what gets that thing kicking.

When a message resonates enough to make people question their own mind, it sparks an organic curiosity, and there's just nothing like it. It's a force you can't compete with, and it actually ends up making your life a whole lot easier as a creator. All that energy you would've put into doing stupid things like getting models to wear orange t-shirts is now replaced with energy the audience is ready, willing, and able to give up themselves. If you get a whiff of apple pie, your nose will be compelled to look for more. It's just how the body works. Your message should be that enticing.

One day me and my mom were watching a video of Mariah Carey from the early 90s. She had those big permed curls and a skin-tight dress that made it hard to believe her tiny frame could belt out such a fierce voice.

"I remember when this first came out," my mom said. "All I was thinking is, who *is* this girl?"

Do people ask that after they see what you've made? They should. People should look around after they get a taste and start wondering, *what just happened? Where did this person come from? How do I find more?* You'd be surprised at how much humans like a little challenge, particularly those of us in this age. We're the generation of the search engine, remember? We find pleasure in digging. We love taking a small message that resonated, popping it into a search engine, and uncovering a world of other messages like it. It's satisfying. It can make us feel like we've found our own little treasure trove. And again, this is a feeling your audience gets that is *entirely separate* from anything you have control over. Stop thinking that getting people to love you is about tricking or convincing them into doing anything. It's just about resonating enough that they will want to do it themselves.

What's the last message that made you go digging for more? How did it make you feel when you found more of it? Think about one of your greasy finger moments. Maybe a selfie with a celebrity you were shy to ask for but did anyway? Maybe a line you waited in for longer than you usually do, but it was worth it? A YouTube binge where you made sure to clock off every video on the side? They say your character is who you are when no one's looking, and when audiences are forming no one's looking either. These actions happen under the seams. They happen because people manage to make time to indulge searching for more as an act of genuine leisure. It might not translate into likes, it might not translate into followers. But for the love of god, as you build this audience, even if you can't see it right away, don't underestimate the extent humans are willing to explore the massive complexities of the world just to find the bits and pieces that matter to them.

Class ended, and people walked up to Lamott to give their last goodbye. I had already decided I would just walk straight to the car. I had found peace with what happened, but I was still a little embarrassed. I felt like coming up to her again would just be unnecessary. But as I was walking towards the door, I realized I might not ever see her again. So I stood again in the line, this time with my coat in my hand. Not a pen, not a paper. And when it was my turn I made sure I locked eyes and I reached for her hand and just said:

"Thank you."

She gripped it firmly and said thank you back, and I know she meant it and I knew this is all there was left to say. She did her part, and I was doing mine. She pulsed her heart into her work well enough that I was able to feel my own. This is the dance of art. *This is engagement.* This leads me to the most powerful punch in the pack, the third part of what engagement really is, which is represented in the telling of this story itself. *Sharing.*

One of the main reasons why I don't think I could ever feel ill-hearted about my first true love is because of a group called *A Tribe Called Quest*. This lover and I would scream their lyrics and bounce around in my car so much that it shook as we drove. I don't know what was more dangerous, screaming those lyrics at the top of our lungs at 90mph or falling in that deep of a love. Their sound, with the sass and confidence of Phife Dawg, mixed with the talented ear of Q-tip, made songs that epitomized the jazzy-funky, golden era of hip-hop. Many of which were sampled from this other guy I mentioned earlier, James Brown.

As the rhythms played, I could just feel the bond between us getting carved inside of me with the same permanence of a tattoo. I knew this music would connect us forever, even if we ever went our separate ways. Eventually we did, and after the break up the music still traveled through my arteries with the same ease. I don't know if it reminded me of him as much as it reminded me of my happiest times. Either way, I was grateful that the charm of the beats still worked.

It had been years, and the day Phife Dawg died I was in another relationship, but as soon as the news hit that morning I just had to text my ex even though I hadn't spoken to him in months.

"Phife is dead :(" I sent.

"Who are you texting?" My new boyfriend asked. I was still in bed and he was laying next to me. I told him I had to text my, erm, friend and let him know that Phife died.

He saw the name on my phone and said, "You're texting your ex in my bed?!"

Whoops. He didn't like *A Tribe Called Quest,* and he definitely didn't like my ex. Needless to say, we broke up a few months later.

Sharing is the part of engagement where a resonating message turns into more than just a movie or a book. This is the part where it transforms from a piece of media or art into the thing that the people in that boardroom meeting could only freaking dream of: an interpersonal, highly-valued, long-lasting bond. There is no orange t-shirt in the nature of the freaking universe that's going to trick people into this type of engagement. To do this, it has to be real.

The first two parts (keeping and looking for more) plant the seed, but the engagement of sharing is where you get to watch this thing grow. If one person tells another person about your message, you get a clump. If they tell more people, it becomes a cluster. If it keeps happening, over a period of time, it becomes a fully bloomed audience. It becomes popular enough that it lives as a separate, dynamic idea, and ideas don't die.

Think about it. When something resonates, isn't your gut reaction to share it with someone who would love it? I couldn't even finish watching a full episode of *Orange Is The New Black* before I told my mom she had to watch it. And she couldn't finish one episode until she had to run off and tell me. Audiences build off of *that*. That urge to yap. That's all it is. An invisible compulsion to testify to the world that you found something you love (or even something you hate) and everyone must know.

Keep. Dig. Share. Keep. Dig. Share. What a darling little pattern, no? This is how word has always gotten around in our society, but with the internet, we could not be better set up for it. Just like in the real world, most of the *real* engagement on social media happens in the parts we can't see. It doesn't happen in the likes or the followers. It happens behind tiny doors and little rooms. Go through your messages. What's the last thing you spoke about? Why? What's the difference between the things you share privately versus the things you share publicly? What matters more? You need to start asking yourself these questions. Study the relationship between the things you share and why you do it.

This will help you figure out how people can share your stuff more, because I'm not going to lie to you kid, if you show ten people your message and none of them share it with a friend— Not one?—you need to start all over again. I'm serious. Go back to the drawing board and think about it again from the start. You can't eat by planting a seed that doesn't grow.

That's what the people in that boardroom were too terrified to hear. They wanted quick, simple fixes to make their problems go away. And danger is amongst the people who ignore the bonafide methods of engagement. In today's retention-starved economy, we just don't have that kind of time. This doesn't have to be a hard pill to swallow if we just address it now. Hell, I think it's good news. Finally we can stop treating the population like mindless blobs and start approaching each other for what we really are—which, sure, might be a confused, lost and desperate people, but still—conscious beings nonetheless.

CHAPTER 13

How A Message Spreads

Let's take more of a technical look at how a message spreads, so you don't lose your shit when you pour your heart into something and *The New York Times* doesn't call you the next day. Before you curl up into a ball because you take my advice and no one but your mom shows up to the first show, just hear me out, okay? There's a process to the way a message spreads, and if you can see it clearly, you'll realize that mom clapping alone from the front row means everything is actually going according to plan. There is a pattern to the development of an audience. You can study and map it out as a journey through four particular developmental stages. It looks like this:

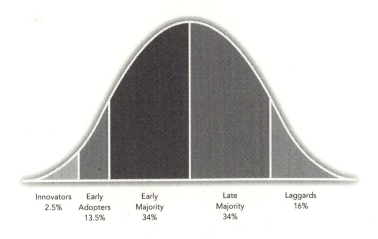

Innovators 2.5% Early Adopters 13.5% Early Majority 34% Late Majority 34% Laggards 16%

In order for an idea to spread, it needs to start with the innovator (creative/entrepreneur). That's you. Congrats. You are different. Blah. Blah. Blah. You've made something that you want the world to appreciate and of course, try. But since most humans don't like trying new things, the only people who will be willing are going to be these folks called "Early Adopters".

Early Adopters

Early Adopters are people who are willing and eager to try things before everybody else. They make up a small part of the population, but play a role that is just as, if not more so, important than the innovator himself when it comes to getting messages to spread. They're responsible for the social adoption of things as simple as scrunchies and as massive as toilet paper. (Yes. There was actually a time where someone had to be brave enough to try toilet paper for the first time in order for it to catch on.)

Early Adopters don't wait for something to be recommended in order for them to try it. To the contrary, on their own, they scout the world for items, trinkets, and messages they find interesting with their bare hands. They will look under rocks, shop at thrift stores. They'll read a book someone threw away, and give a song that has 0 plays a try. Chances are, if you're reading this book, you're probably an Early Adopter yourself. It's rare that people who fit into the "innovator" category don't also fit into the Early Adopter one as well.

Early Adopters are the gate-keepers of cool, and the fortune tellers of what will be the next big thing. Nothing slips into the mainstream without their approval. They are the friends that rub in your face that they heard the new Drake song way before you. They had the new iPhone before you even knew another one came out. These people are serious about being ahead of everyone else. Their whole identity is based on it. If culture was a party, they'd be the guy who can get you on the list so you don't have to wait in line. They want to feel responsible for keeping tabs on the things the rest of the world eventually falls in love with, and it's because in a lot of ways—they are. "Cool" really just ends up being a mashup of what they say it is and what they predict it will be. Who pays them for this? Nobody.

It's a gift that human nature gave the species, that stems from a strange combination of curiosity and the need to feel unique, separate, and dare I say, better.

So what happens is that the Early Adopters scatter their strong and thoughtful opinions all over their social circles and it's through them, not the brand, not the majority, not even the inventor!—that audiences are built. It happens from multiple individual conversations that happen at fancy parties, first dates, and expensive brunches. They're also happening on social media 24/7. "You have to watch this new show." "You have to download this new app." Early Adopters are here to tell us what we have to try. They want the social credit for sharing it with you first.

Each of us have a little Early Adopter in us. Most people make an effort to be the first to try specific things like hair products, coffee flavors, or vegan recipes. But a full blown Early Adopter makes trying things first into a lifestyle. It's from their recommendations that cause ideas/products/messages to balloon up into mainstream conversations and appeal to the folks who come next: the Early Majority.

The Early Majority

These people won't listen to your mixtape because you,

the innovator, asked. They'll listen to it because one of their Early Adopter friends said it was good. They trust the friend. They don't trust you, and as the inventor you have to understand this and not take it personal. It will be a waste of your time to try to build trust directly with the Early Majority, and I know it's tempting. They're a big group. But they already have a selection of sources they trust, and they don't plan to let you in anytime soon. They don't have the same appetite to try new things as much as the Early Adopters. That door is shut. As an inventor, you need to be clever and instead of banging on the door like a madman, activate a line of trust they already have established. Work around the door. Appeal to people who already have a key (the Early Adopters) and you'll be able to walk right in.

Once you're inside, you only have one job to do. Impress them. Resonate. It's your time to shine. The Early Adopter is taking a risk by recommending you. You've got to be great. More than one reputation is on the line here. If the recommendation goes well and you appeal, then you, my friend, have another mouth. A mouth that's going to say great things about you, because even though the Early Majority doesn't try new things, they still talk just as much as everybody else. The people they tell will be the next group on the list, the Late Majority.

The Late Majority

These people are the sheepish of the sheep but you've gotta love them for it. They are the opposite of Early Adopters in the sense that the second something gets on the mainstream train, the Late Majority hops on with enthusiasm and the Early Adopters jump off with disgust. If culture was a party, the Late Majority, well—they'd be late. They missed the main act but the good news is they still count because they bought a ticket anyway. And you know why I find them to be so charming? They'll still enjoy themselves even if the Early Adopters don't think it's cool. The Late Majority are the people who buy the Forever 21 accessories that an Early Adopter designed and sold in a trendy pop-up boutique two years ago. The Late Majority sends you memes that look like they were made during the beginning of the internet. And they don't have an ego complex about any of it.

People get googly eyed at the majority section of the chart, both early and late, because it seems like they have a lot money to offer. What most people try to do is cheat through the audience building pattern by stealing and buying airtime from the thickest parts of other mass audiences. Most people only care about getting exposed to all those eyeballs. Quantity over quality. That's their motto. But avoiding the edges of this chart doesn't usually end well. You can't aim smack dab in the middle of the population and expect to grip any quality attention. It's like trying to sell lemonade to a pack of stampeding water buffalo. Herds don't listen. They can't listen. They're herds. None of them are going to stop running to hear what you have to say, they're too busy keeping up, running, scrolling with the rest. They are majorities, and majorities don't think for themselves. They follow. To build an audience on your own, stop trying to cheat. Become attractive to leaders (Early Adopters). Get them yapping about you and your job is done, seriously.

The Laggards

Next on this chart is another group I don't really have to tell you about, but I will anyway since I find this part of the population to be so charming: The Laggards. This is the grandpa who asks you to please get him a cell phone but it doesn't need texting or any of that fancy stuff. These people are not concerned with coolness whatsoever. They buy simply because they need something for its function. They are not late to the party, they show up when the party's over. In fact, they didn't even know there was a party, they just want to send out this letter, via fax if possible. These are the people who give the camcorder and magazine porn industry just enough money to feed on right before they become completely extinct. I find this market to be both entertaining and mysterious. Even though they are small markets, they can be just as powerful and profitable as the Early Adopter market, ranging in technically the same size but with a different type of momentum. Where the Early Adopter market rises and swells with a feverish growth, the Laggard market dwindles down onto its death, which usually matches up to the literal death of its customers.

And this, my creative friend, is how ideas and audiences grow and die. Two Questions. Does this make you feel better? And, how do you make this information work for you?

First off, save yourself some time and money and stop trying to talk to the majorities. They can't hear you, and to be honest, you don't need them. That part of the population is overrated in terms of its buying power and loyalty, and on top of that, it's shrinking. The internet is making a world where "majorities" don't really exist in the same way they used to. In fact, they never really existed. It was a myth. When there were only a few avenues to speak to the masses, it gave us the illusion that there was some type of "majority", and this is what people used to design their messages around. TV shows, ads, movies, books were made for this "majority" that was literally as ambiguous as a gray shadow. This is why so many messages and ads pre-internet felt so conforming and insensitive. They were.

They made a lot of money and got so much attention

not because they were any *good* per se, but because there were such few choices! You couldn't just pull up any song anytime you wanted. You couldn't just watch a show because you felt like it. The consumer had to wait, sometimes long periods of time for these types of entertainment, making the relationship they had with it totally different than the one we have today. Where teens of that era had to arrange their schedules around what time the radio would be playing the Beatles, teens now have to strategically ignore constant tempting requests of entertainment just so they can focus on the ones they like the most.

The internet has cracked the majority into a billion tiny pieces, and it has entirely shifted the axis of the marketplace of art and entertainment. When humans have a more democratized chance to choose what we want, we get to see the true shape of demand, unfiltered. And what it really looks like is a nervous system made up of tiny niches. We, on our own, through social platforms, have created clusters and enclaves of micro-cultures. Fringes upon fringes. And what we've learned to discover about ourselves is that each of us actually has our own unique tastes. Consumers today are spoiled rotten with so many options, we've had no choice but to get picky. Each of us digitally hand-carve individual roads of preference with the help of our curiosity and ability to navigate reviews. When these thin roads collide with other people, we form our own very specific, authentic worlds via social media. We make identities and friends, fans and followers. Thus, a robust, profitable niche is born.

The word "niche" scares people because when they hear it they think it means "small" or "unpopular". They envision performing in front of ten people who are picking their boogers at a cheap venue with broken chairs. They think going niche means making certain financial and personal sacrifices as a way to settle—as a way to be more "realistic" about the impractical chances of genuine, thriving success. But it's such a poor misconception. As I propose the power of a niche to you, I am not asking you to snip at your dreams. No ideas need to be scratched. No financial opportunities need to be squandered. You can take your creative visions as far as you want them to go. Niche markets will not interfere with them. They will only make them more feasible.

Niches are not about size as much as they are about detail. They don't gather people through the shallow enticement of popularity. That's so pre-internet. They gather people from something deeper. From agreed psychographics and shared values. This difference in how people come together bloom organic and richer followings. Their buying power is sturdier, stronger, and their love for you is more loyal than a "majority" could ever be. Author and thought leader Kevin Kelley wrote a famous essay back in 2008 about his theory on gathering "1,000 true fans":

HOW A MESSAGE SPREADS

To be a successful creator you don't need millions. You don't need millions of dollars or millions of customers, millions of clients or millions of fans. To make a living as a craftsperson, photographer, musician, designer, author, animator, app maker, entrepreneur, or inventor you need only thousands of true fans.

A true fan is defined as a fan that will buy anything you produce. These diehard fans will drive 200 miles to see you sing; they will buy the hardback and paperback and audible versions of your book; they will purchase your next figurine sight unseen; they will pay for the "best-of" ... version of your free youtube channel; they will come to your chef's table once a month. If you have roughly a thousand true fans like this (also known as super fans), you can make a living — if you are content to make a living but not a fortune.

He goes on to say:

The big corporations, the intermediates, the commercial producers, are all under-equipped and ill suited to connect with these thousand true fans. They are institutionally unable to find and deliver niche audiences and consumers. That means the long tail is wide open to you, the creator. You'll have your one-in-a-million true fans to yourself. And the tools for connecting keep getting better, including the recent innovations in social media. It has never been easier to gather 1,000 true fans around a creator, and never easier to keep them near.

You don't need a big following, you just need a real one. You need—like Kevin Kelly puts it— "true fans," people who will talk about you with approving words to each other over and over again. Having that information already de-risks your chances of failing, but understanding how much power resonance has on top of this practically turns it into a formula. Because when you resonate, it doesn't matter where people fall on this chart. It has nothing to deal with them being an Early Adopter or a Laggard; a vegan or liberal. All that matters is that those people are human.

But the reason why I wanted to show you this is because there's logic in honing your focus on Early Adopters. They're more open minded about trying new stuff, and this will help you save so much energy and time. You needed this chart in order to see that. But more importantly, don't freak out when you publish something and all you hear at first are whispers. Give it some time, trust the process and let it unravel, because have you ever been in a room with a thousand people whispering?

It's extremely loud.

CHAPTER 14

Branding and Resonating

They know not to come up to me. They can tell I'm from around here. I'm talking about the men who sell knock-off designer bags on Canal Street in Manhattan. Everyone in New York abides to this unspoken distance you're supposed to keep between people when walking down the street. But on Canal Street, there are men and women who will inch up close to the tourists who don't know about this golden distance and whisper, "Chanel handbag. Chanel, Gucci." That is the call for the journey. If you show interest, they will pull you aside and show you their impressive inventory of impersonated designer bags. Louis Vuitton, Gucci, Chanel. They are bright and propped up. Stiff and deceptive enough to delude you, the same way they will delude others as you wear one.

New Yorkers are obsessed with brands. In fact, New York *is* a brand. People actually fly here to buy bags and shirts with our subway maps printed on them. More than once I've seen tourists stop New York City police officers and ask them for a picture. They gawk at the yellow cabs that zoom down the street, and will absolutely lose it if they stumble upon one of those carriages people ride around Central Park in like they're all romantic, though really the horse is old and sick looking.

If you zoom-in on the everyday people of New York City, we are just as obsessed with brands as people are with us. Part of keeping up the brand of New York City is keeping up with the brands of everything else. In middle school, the pressure to wear name brand things was so intense, kids everywhere would rob or steal—do the unspeakable—just to have a shirt that said "Rocawear" on it. Being that most of us were too young to care about design, it didn't matter how ugly a thing was as long as it had one of the ten acceptable logos. Even if we didn't like it; even if it didn't fit over our awkward, smelly middle school bodies. One year the most hideous sneakers I've ever seen were for sale. They were on the watch list for every pubescent kid in Brooklyn who cared about their social life.

They were called the "Dub-zeros", and apparently, they were an exclusive release to the Jordan sneaker collection. I knew these kinds of things not because I cared, but because I had to. It's the only way I wouldn't get harassed in school. I heard about them through whispers amongst the halls as we went in and out of class. They were coming out this Saturday and everybody already had a plan to get them. I didn't know how they looked. I didn't know if I liked them or not. All I knew is that if I didn't show up with them on Monday, my social rank would be knocked down a notch or two. I had to start brainstorming—now.

My parents never bought me Jordans. They didn't see the point. Too much to pay for growing feet, they said. I had no empathy for their thrifty parental logic as a thirteen-year-old, so I'd try to work around it in the most creative ways I could. I held off on asking for a pair for a year as a method to accumulate what I thought would work as "credit". This way I could build some wiggle room without getting an immediate "No" when I asked. It didn't work.

One time I got impatient and used scissors to cut the tongues out of my everyday sneakers so they'd be left with no choice but to buy new ones. "See? They're broken," I said as I held them up to my mom with my head bowed low. She rolled her eyes and called my dad. "Yes. It appears there's intentional damage done to them, Joe." I know my parents made an effort to sound civil around each other after the divorce, but Jesus. They were talking about me like I was a specimen. They sent me to school the next day with my laces strapped super tight so that the loose tongues would stay in place.

I needed to think carefully about how I was going to get the Dub-Zeros. Terrified, I asked my mom if she wanted to walk down Fulton this weekend. Fulton is where a lot of stores are in Brooklyn. My plan was to stumble across the Dub-Zeros and make my case while we were in the store. I'd rant about how long it's been since I had new sneakers, and if I had to beg, so be it.

We walked into a Foot Locker. Of course, they were right there on display, dead center, within a few steps of the entrance. Mens, kids, and baby sizes all lined up next to each other like one big happy family. "See, these were the ones I was telling you about, Mom."

"Those? Those are ugly," she said.

I looked down at them. She was right. They looked absolutely pitiful. I couldn't find any charm in them whatsoever. They were hard. They looked uncomfortable. But they were the ones.

"Can I get these in a size 7 please?" I was so anxious, my question trailed off at the end like smoke.

"They're sold out," the Foot Locker guy said.

The sad part is I kind of knew this would be the case, but felt I had to try anyway.

"Do you have a 6?" I asked, still trembling.

My mom interrupted. "Alex, you can't fit a 6!"

I shot an annoyed glance at her, then gave the guy a pleading look. "Let me check," he said.

"Mom, I probably *could* fit a 6, okay? If I wear thin socks." I mumbled the last part under my breath. At that point, she realized I was completely delusional and let me stare at the other shoes. The Foot Locker guy walked back. There was no box in his hand.

"The only thing we have is a 4.5," he said as he leaned over the counter.

My mom was about to turn around and walk out, but I wasn't quite ready. How could I dare to show my face Monday morning without these damn Dub-Zeros?

Herein lies the reason why I'm telling you this story. As a young growing girl who wore a size 7, I seriously asked the man at the Foot Locker if he could get me the size 4.5, please. He looked down at my feet. My mom looked down at my feet. I looked down at my feet. We all thought the same thing.

"Okay, I'll go get them," he said, ignoring my mom's stare.

When he came back, I tried. I really tried to squeeze my foot into a shoe that could only fit about three of my toes. Four if I clenched. All this to avoid the smirks and giggles of Monday morning. Yet here I was—getting exactly that.

When people hear the word "brand", they quickly think about the colors or symbols a rich company uses to represent itself. It's a good guess, but that's not really it. Brands are invisible. Any part of it you can see, smell, or hear is designed to ultimately steer the way you *feel*.

It wasn't the colors of the Dub-Zeros that made me stuff my foot into a shoe like that. It was the fact that enough kids went so crazy for the *feeling* of wearing the same sneakers that an all-time basketball champion wore, that I felt pressured into being crazy about it too. You were there in the 90s, weren't you? Liking Michael Jordan wasn't just for people who liked basketball, it was for *everybody*. You bought the sneakers even if you couldn't dribble a ball, and you wore the Bull's jerseys even if you weren't from Chicago. The MJ super fans were so passionate about their obsession, it made the rest of us get excited too. People jump on bandwagons because, think about it—there's a freaking band, rolling around in a wagon. That shit's fun.

But the point I'm trying to make is that branding is not a business thing, it's a social thing. Which is why as an artist, it shouldn't intimidate you. If brands are just feelings, then it means you don't have to stress over colors, logos, or whatever box you think you'll need to fit into in order to market yourself. Just start thinking about the feelings you want your work to be responsible for, and use those to create multiple impressions of resonance. Do this enough times and it'll give the logos and the colors more meaning. Jingles, logos—those just help remind people subconsciously of the feeling you gave them last time. But if you don't make enough valuable, resonating impressions, they won't work as strongly as you'd like them to. Most people start this process backwards, thinking colors and logos are the things that will make their brand "click". There's just no way. The founder of Nike, Phil Knight, bought the Nike logo for $35. He made it worth tens of billions of dollars by working with a team that devised a feeling of accomplishment and athleticism to be triggered once it's seen. Brands—I'm telling you, they're invisible.

So resonate again and again with people over time, and it will build a brand by default. It's not an easy process, but it is a simple one. And stay focused because you don't have as much control as you think you do. Brands are more than just the feelings *you* want to be responsible for, they're the feelings you'll *have* to be responsible for either way. Whoever it attracts will be how other people decide whether or not they want to be associated with it. Your brand is not you. Your brand is your fans. Part of how we decide whether or not to try listening to a new artist or buying from a new designer is by paying attention to who else is doing it. If they're people we'd like to be associated with, then we're more inclined to be a fan.

See, building a brand is like taping a tiny message into a sailboat and flicking it off into the ocean. All you can do is cross your fingers and hope it gets perceived the way you originally planned. Because once the people have it, it will be theirs, and you'll have to work with whatever happens next. The reason you don't need to box yourself in is because other people will do that for you. The right people might hate it. The wrong people might love it. You might've outgrown it by the time it takes wind. A lot can happen en route. Expect to exercise tremendous patience and strategy until you get it right. People are simple minded. They pigeon hole. Once they think they've figured you out, they keep that idea of you just because it's human to do so.

This is the speck on the window many brands I've worked with keep trying to scrub off. I have to keep telling them, no. That speck is not coming off. This is just how it works. This is why I discourage people from trying to be everything to everyone at the same time. You're just making the work harder for yourself when you do that. Don't focus on being liked, focus on being understood. If you have enough grit (or hire a professional) you eventually get better about how to set sail to get the boat where you want. It took over a decade for Michael Jackson's little sister to become Janet. It took half a dozen hits for Jimmy from Degrassi to become Drake.

It all comes down to perception. Perception is the real currency our culture runs on now. These micro-cultures on social media are forming because *there has never been this much pressure to try to show the world who you are.* What you listen to, what you wear, the places you go, the food you eat. These are things we've gotten accustomed to sharing online as a way to communicate, position ourselves in social circles, and, unfortunately, gauge our self-worth. And this laser-guided focus everyday people have on creating a perception of themselves for their online audience of "followers" or "friends" or whatever, has influenced buying behavior in a way we've never seen it before.

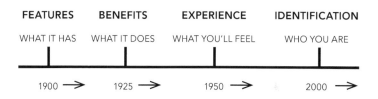

Before the internet age, we cared more about what things had or what things did for us. And even though we still care about that stuff now, purchase behavior is showing that today more than ever, we're buying things as a way to affirm *who we are*. It's now become an identity thing. We're more willing to spend money on goods and services which make a statement about our ideology and perspective on life. We need songs, books, clothes, and movies that will help properly represent ourselves when it's time to go out there in the big black hole of the internet and claim our stance. How else are we going to be able to attract the right friends and lovers? How else are we going to dig up some confidence in this digital world that is overbearingly competitive? We need messages that will make us feel both *proud* to be who we are and *crystal clear* of who we are. The vegans need stuff that will make them feel proud to be vegans. They minimalists need stuff that will make them feel proud for being minimalists. Your message, whether subtly or not, needs to amplify the idea people have *about themselves,* and flatter that idea enough so they feel naturally motivated to buy it.

You see this clearly with the poets, authors, and artists who have a big following but aren't necessarily the highest-grade. You aren't going crazy. The reason they got popular is because they help the people in their audience *feel* like they're into art, which can make just as much money as an audience who actually *is* into art. There's a difference between people who like poetry and people who *want* to like poetry. But people who *want* to like poetry will spend just as much money as a person who actually does like it, because they think it's important to be perceived that way. You see? It's not just you. Our culture is set up so that we're all in this game of perception.

Now, of course, do not dilute the quality of your work! That's far from what I'm proposing. Stay strong. Stay potent, and always focus on resonating. I just want you to have a clear understanding as to why certain things catch on and others don't. It's not hard for us to buy into things that will help validate and confirm for us that we can be perceived as we wish to be.

Typically, products/services are in demand when they offer some sort of practical and functional purpose; adding convenience to the flow of our everyday lives. We buy washing machines to make washing clothes easier. We buy toasters because they brown our waffles and bread with perfection. But when you're selling what you're selling, my friend—this art of yours—you are positioning yourself outside the boundaries of typical supply and demand, and entering a more elusive kind of economy. As a creative, when you go into the market place, you have to understand that you aren't selling your art the way most of the other ways people sell products and appliances. I know people like us think we "need" art to survive, but when we put our personal philosophy aside, we don't "need" it in the same way we need milk or rice. This means that for people to be compelled to buy from you, you must make something they really *want*. Something that will make them *feel*. Something that will confirm for them that they're the type of person that should be into what you do because it lines up with them philosophically. How can you help people do this? Don't beg people to listen to your music or read your book. Figure out what it will it mean to be a fan of yours first, and people will have an easier time making that decision for themselves.

Strong brands are miles ahead of you when it comes to asking these types of questions. They know you can get a decent pair of sneakers for $70 dollars, but Jordan decides to sell millions of them at $150+ a pop because they created an identity around it. You are not paying for sneakers, you're paying for a particular type of acceptance. Because it doesn't make any logical sense to spend that much on sneakers when you can get the same physical quality for cheaper. But who needs sense? Humans, when given the privilege to live in an economically developed society, don't need to make sense. Rationality is a tool for survivors. Coming up with excuses to brainwash yourself into buying a $2,000 bag when you can get one that works just as well for $30—that's for the thriving class.

As the economy is changing, the idea of the brand has never had more power in the way the consumer makes their decision to purchase. In the past fifteen years, 52% of companies have disappeared because they kept focusing on which vehicle to reach the new American consumer instead of choosing to see that the new American consumer *is* the vehicle. Think about it. With our phones, we now have all the tools (influence, networks, platforms) to do a large part of the marketing for you. The brands who will succeed understand that instead of running in circles and yelling, they just need to focus on making it easy for people to express who they are. Unlike the other brands that try to make us feel dumb, the successful ones just need to make really clear what being a fan of their stuff means. The rest of us are smart enough to take it from there.

The brand is the artistic side of the business because it's all about feelings. Even if you're selling something as essential as water bottles—actually, *especially* if you are selling water bottles—you can't expect to sell them because water is important. It's not the water that you're selling, it's the *feeling* people get while carrying that water, and what they think it communicates to the world about their identity. This may not make any objective sense, I know, but it makes all the socially-insecure, validating-craved human sense in the world. And that's why, as a creative, instead of being intimidated by entering the market place, you should actually feel right at home.

CONCLUSION

Sometimes I forget how many people know about what I've done until I have to do something in person. Many things haven't changed. After all these years, I'm still the girl who feels most at home in front of her computer. Even now, I'm my most peaceful self staring at all the buttons on the side of the screen. Together we've come so far. And the audiences I've helped build, even the ones that range into the hundreds of thousands, can seem modest from that angle, because when you interact with them behind a screen, there's no sound.

That's why this one spring day I was startled to hear hundreds, if not thousands, of voices echoing off the walls of an auditorium. I had been invited to speak at a fancy event but wasn't prepared for this much energy and enthusiasm. Backstage, everybody in the green room was yelling over each other about who would need to stand where. Photos were being snapped. Makeup brushed on faces. The whole room just felt so considerably important. Amidst all this tumult, I became suspicious. Something wasn't allowing me to believe I could be responsible for creating anything that could generate this much *noise*.

I tried to embrace it anyway. It's at events like this that I practice my ability to human. I harp on the dangers of technology and how they desensitize us only because I've single handedly watched how they've impaired me. Connecting quietly online is one thing, but in person? I'm overwhelmed. It's on days like this that I try to combat that by looking into faces and seeing the texture of people's skin. I like noticing the eyelash glue on women's eyes, and the actual shape of men's heads. There are smells, gestures, smirks I encounter in real time that the internet doesn't really let me have.

In the corner of the room was a young photographer. She looked like she had just got out of high school. There was optimism in her cheeks.

"Alex! I follow you!" she said.

I smiled and said hello. We took a few pictures, and then she told me how she was in college studying medicine, which was a shame. I could tell she wanted to be studying something else. She had hand sewn patches on her camera strap, a pair of beat up converse on her feet, and a tattoo floating on her arm that looked like in a few years it'd be hidden amongst more.

"You want to be a doctor?" I asked, anticipating her reply.

She laughed. No, she said, but her parents ... well, they were paying for school. Then she promptly changed the subject to tell me about her business ideas. How maybe after school, eight years from now, she could use her photography skills to take pictures and hopefully build an audience. I could've gotten lost in her eyes, how they glistened with possibilities. She smelled like ambition, and the camera was still hanging from her neck when she looked at me and said:

> "I just want to help people like you did. I want to make the world a better place."

Just then a security guard tapped my shoulder to escort me to the stage. It was time to go. I became slightly nervous, anxious, not only because now I had to speak, but because I didn't get a chance to tell her what I really wanted to say. If I'd had a little more time I would've said that I didn't grow an audience from trying to make the world a better place, and that she shouldn't either.

I'm not 100% sure, but I think why what I did worked was because my life experiences had harvested somewhat of an emotional hairball inside me that at one point my body just forced itself to gag out. Sure, I started all of this wanting recognition, "fame", and to "help people", but I

CONCLUSION

don't think any of that is actually what ended up making people listen to me. And it's definitely not what made any of this experience feel worth it. What really happened is that I felt like if I'd allowed one more day of silence, one more day of cooperation with the masking of my thoughts or feelings, I was going to die. I shared myself not because I wanted to make anyone else feel better. I was doing it for me.

What the years have shown me, is that building an audience has very little to deal with the audience itself. Instead, it has to deal with a nerve you either have or don't have, to try to be you in the fullest way possible, no matter how messy or flawed. To be alive, vulnerable, passionate—in front of others. That energy is ten times more magnetic than the energy in morality, purity, or perfection. Audiences form the most successfully when the artist's incentive is selfish, not righteous.

There's a lecture one of my favorite philosophers, Alan Watts, has where he says:

> "Sometimes when we try to do good for others ... it's amazingly destructive because it's full of conceit. How do you know what's good for other people? How do you know what's good for you?"

These are important questions, because they help us face the fact that the world we live in is full of people who don't need help as much as they need *acceptance*. We don't want someone to give us a hand so much as we want someone to give us a hug. Trying to "help", even though it's an innocent and honorable intention, implies a hierarchy, an assumption that you would even know where to start.

Watts continues with a joke:

> "'Kindly let me help you or you'll drown' said the monkey putting the fish safely on the tree."

See, if I had a few more minutes I would've told that girl I admired her passion and desire to make things—that impulse would take her far—but I would've also said not to get lost thinking about how it can help other people. We do that when we want to be safe, when we think our ambitions are too self-indulgent to take part in. When we think it will be easier to enforce authority, instead of express authenticity.

When things were looking impossible in my early twenties, I wanted to give up on becoming an artist. Nothing was working, and I just felt disgusted with my need to express myself. I thought something about it was wrong, or evil. I wanted to back out and do something a little less selfish for the world. Something that would seem safe and normal enough for people to get without asking me a million dumb questions. I went to my friends house to complain.

"Maybe I'll just be a librarian," I told her. She was zoned out on the computer and hadn't looked up until I said that. When I did, she lit a cigarette, blew smoke from the corner of her mouth, and said "Alex—you're not going to be a fucking librarian."

Which is along the lines of what I would've told the girl backstage. I'd freak her out a bit, nudge her in the shoulder, raise my eyebrows and use the S word. "Be a little *selfish*," I'd say. Think about you! What do *you* want? I would've asked her to articulate the things she wished to tell her controlling parents, or whatever dude she was banging in school. I would've encouraged her to share the colorful, sloppy, contradictory thoughts she has about life and love through her photography. I would've tried to show her the beauty in her own opinions, her ability to think for herself, and how that alone would be enough.

When Elizabeth Gilbert published her internationally recognized memoir, *Eat, Pray Love,* it didn't catch wind because she wanted to make the world a better place, though you can argue it did that anyway. Millions of women cried over the pages, laughed through the stories, and festered up courage. They took exotic trips, left toxic husbands, and found better lives for themselves. The book made a positive impact not because it meant to, but because Gilbert felt like she was going to explode if she didn't share what happened to her. She urges her readers to see this pattern too:

When people say to me I want to write a book and I say 'Why do you want to write it?' ... the first thing they say is 'I want to help people.' The first thing I do is [think] 'Oh dear god, please do not let me read that book'... The book I want to read ... is the book ... about the thing that you are most excited about! I want to read the book about the thing that makes you want to get up in the morning ... I want to read the book that you had to write because you couldn't NOT do it. I want to see the creative project you did because something in you was so restless and relentless that it just wouldn't leave you alone ... [that's how], you're going to help me."

The world does not need another hero. It does not need another person that we must bend our necks back in order to look up at. We are tired of high horses. They exhaust us, and make us feel more alone. Don't go out there hoping you're going to fix the world, or make us into better people. You're only human, just like us. You don't have that power.

The only lightswitch you control in this life is yourself, and it's up to you whether you want to leave it off or on. I'm not saying you have to show us everything. By all means, keep some mystery. Keep what makes you spark awe. But the parts you do show should let us know that you're fully aware that you're just here, floating on a ball in outer space like we are. You don't know what's really going on, none of us do.

All we know is that everyday we're here, we get the privilege to feel things, good and bad. Breaths go short. Necks get hot. Arms sway. Lungs laugh. In this sublime world, not only is there so much to do, but there is so much we can feel *together*. We can hold onto each other energetically, through our songs and our letters—our art, as we try to make sense of it all. Through the things we make and share, we can giggle together at our hypocrisy, our tendencies to fall into stupid situations, and our constant drive to seek out better ones.

Will you show us how you really feel living on this planet with the rest of us? How human you are? Because if you do, when we look at you, we won't see a person on a high horse. We won't see an expert. We won't see a person who has figured it all out. When you show us something from deep inside of yourself, the world will automatically seem like a better place to us, because it'll feel like beneath all those piles of expectations and foolishness life has given us to dig through, we'll have finally found what we've been desperately seeking to find all along: a person who gets it. A friend.

Notes

Chapter 1
Leo Tolstoy quotes from *What is Art?*, 1897
James Baldwin quote from *LIFE Magazine,* May 24, 1963

Chapter 3
Marina Abramovic quote from *Electricity Passing Through,* by The Louisiana Channel

Chapter 4
Statistic on cell phone related car crashes from:
http://www.businessinsider.com/cell-phones-causing-car-crashes-and-deaths-2015-5

Chapter 8
Chris Rock quote from *Never Scared*, 2004

Chapter 10
Anton Chekov quote from *The Seagull*, 1897, translated 1986
Aristotle quote from *Poetics*, 335 BC

Chapter 11
Fred Wesley quote from *The Story Of Funk – One Nation Under Groove*, 2014

NOTES

William Shakespeare quote from *The Merchant of Venice*, 1596

Louis Armstrong quote from *Jazz 101: A Complete Guide to Learning and Loving Jazz*, by John F. Szwed, 2000 (https://en.wikiquote.org/wiki/Jazz)

Chapter 13

Kevin Kelly quote from "1,000 True Fans," 2008

Chapter 14

Statistics on consumers from: https://www.bcg.com/publications/2014/marketing-center-consumer-customer-insight-how-millennials-changing-marketing-forever.aspx

Chapter 15

Alan Watts quote from his lecture "Why The Urge To Improve Yourself?"

Elizabeth Gilbert quote from "Compassion and Creativity" by SalesForce, 2016

Acknowledgements

Thank you Mom and Dad for finding each other and staying together long enough to have me. A big thank you to Daniel DiPiazza who yelled at me for oh—I don't know—a year or two to get this book out. Thank you to my editor Brian Gresko and my book cover designer Sofia Cope. Lisa Ellevor and Diahann Williams for the photo help.

Thank you to my friends who allow me to be a knucklehead and bother them with a million ideas, a million times a day. Your friendship has helped made this possible. Keep being my friend, please.

ALEX WOLF is an award-winning writer + artist. She lives in Brooklyn, New York.

For more, sign up for her newsletter at:
> www.alexwolf.co

— ♡ —
The stories involving your Dad. It's a palatable backdrop & context that explains your essence. Makes you 8-Dimensional.
↳ Indian restaurant multi

✓ Inspiring.

? Why no visuals?

"If your stuff is so good, then why haven't I seen it yet?" —Lena Waithe
— pg. 49

"I am not your zombie." —54
— pg. 56 | "Eminem + waste his time making messages for perfect people." —p. 68

Authority ⟶ authenticity
help   hug/acceptance
righteous   selfish
hero   human/friend

(?) P. 171 You mention the things women did after reading Eat, Pray, Love. What do you want ppl to do when they read your book?

(?) What's your favorite argument you make in Resonate?

Made in the USA
San Bernardino, CA
24 April 2018